CONTENTS

PREFACE

Swimming is a popular activity, at once a sport, a recreational pursuit and a life-saving skill. It is a well-documented and widespread activity in most countries across the world. Famous swimmers are household names and participating in swimming is second nature to millions. However, there is still a need for many to fully understand the sport, and to improve their techniques and their competitive performances.

Early references to the activity are to be found in the Old Testament, and the first organized national competition is known to have taken place in England in 1869. As a measure of the progress of swimming and its global appeal, the World Swimming Championships of 2005 had more than 2,000 competitors from 157 countries participating in such diverse activities as Swimming, Water Polo, Diving, Open-Water Swimming and Synchronized Swimming.

Recent Government policies relating to education, such as the National Curriculum in England and Wales, have led to a strong lobby for swimming to be included as an entitlement for all children. At the most basic level, every child should have the opportunity to learn a potentially life-saving skill, and to become familiar with an activity that can provide lifelong enjoyment.

The aim of this book is to improve the swimming ability of all readers, young or old, novice or expert. Through a series of chapters that are easy to read and understand, the sport of swimming is explained and the strokes developed, from beginner stages through to advanced competition level. Advice on training, racing and coaching is given, with sample sessions and race strategies from champion swimmers and coaches.

PART I
INTRODUCTION TO SWIMMING

CHAPTER I

THE SPORT – HISTORY, STROKES AND RULES

History

The English are credited with the development of swimming as a competitive sport. By the mid-nineteenth century (around 1840), regular swimming competitions were being held in London's six artificial pools, organized by the National Swimming Society in England. As the sport grew in popularity, many more pools were built, and when a new governing body, the Amateur Swimming Association (ASA), was formed, in 1880, it numbered more than 300 member clubs.

The first modern Olympic Games in 1896 incorporated only four swimming events, three of them Frontcrawl (more commonly known today as Freestyle). The second Olympics, in Paris in 1900, included three highly unusual swimming events: one used an obstacle course; another was a test of underwater swimming endurance; and the third was a 4,000m event, still the longest Olympic swimming event ever. None of the three was ever used in the Olympics again. The first-ever Olympic swimming event was a 100m Freestyle race between three Greek sailors across the Bay of Zea, which started with the rivals jumping from rowing boats. The winner was Ioannis Malokins in 2 minutes and 20 seconds. The Backstroke event was introduced in Paris (1900) and Breaststroke surfaced as an Olympic stroke in 1908 at the London Games. Almost half a century passed before a fourth stroke event, Butterfly, was added, in 1956 at the Melbourne Games. The first indication of the modern race programme emerged in St Louis, in 1904, yet it was still only men competing at this time. For a variety of reasons, women were excluded from swimming in the early years of the modern Olympic Games, and

they raced for the first time only in 1912, in Stockholm. In 1896 and again in 1900, women were not permitted to participate because the developer of the modern Olympics, Baron Pierre de Coubertin, believed in the commonly held assumption of the Victorian era, that women were too frail to engage in competitive sports.

Swimming soon became one of the glamour events of the Olympic Games and today a ticket for an Olympic swimming session is a much sought-after commodity. Exposure through the sport opened up significant opportunities to a number of swimmers, such as Duke Kahanamoku (USA), who won the 1912 and 1920 Freestyle sprint titles. Johnny Weissmuller, the American who became the first to swim under a minute for the 100m Freestyle, is perhaps the most famous pre-Second World War swimmer. His sporting success attracted the attention of Hollywood producers, and he went on to star in the early Tarzan movies. Another film star to start his career in the pool was 1932 Olympic champion Buster Crabbe (better known later as Flash Gordon). Crabbe got his passport to Hollywood by taking the 400m Freestyle title, winning by what he described as 'the tenth of a second that changed my life'.

More recently, Mark Spitz's seven gold medals at the 1972 Munich Games assured his legendary status as a worldwide sporting superstar and, at the 2004 Athens Olympics, American Michael Phelps and Australian Ian Thorpe confirmed their positions as global sporting icons. Incidentally, at those same Athens Games, the Dutch swimmer Pieter Van den Hoogenband's winning time of 48.17 seconds for the Men's 100m Freestyle was more than 1 minute 30 seconds faster than Malokins' efforts in that first-ever Olympic swim.

KEY POINT

The competitive events for Olympic swimming are:

- Freestyle: 50m, 100m, 200m, 400m, 800m (women), 1500m (men)
- Backstroke: 100m, 200m
- Breaststroke: 100m, 200m
- Butterfly: 100m, 200m
- Individual Medley: 200m, 400m
- Relays: 4 × 100m Freestyle, 4 × 100m Medley, 4 × 200m Freestyle

In World, European and Commonwealth competitions, there are also 50m events for Butterfly, Backstroke and Breaststroke.

The Strokes

The evolution of the four competitive strokes is shown in Fig 1.

Freestyle is the most popular stroke. Technically, within the rules, Freestyle competitors may use whatever stroke they like, but freestyle (originally known as frontcrawl) is the quickest. Causes of disqualification are few, but include swimming outside your lane, walking along the bottom of the pool and not touching the wall at the turn or finish.

Backstroke resembles freestyle swimming as far as the alternating movements of arms and legs are concerned. When starting, competitors take their place in the pool facing the wall and holding the starting blocks with both hands. Apart from failing to complete the race on their back, another common cause for disqualification is crossing the 15m mark underwater from the start or turns.

Breaststroke is a fairly complex swimming style, calling for smooth coordination of the

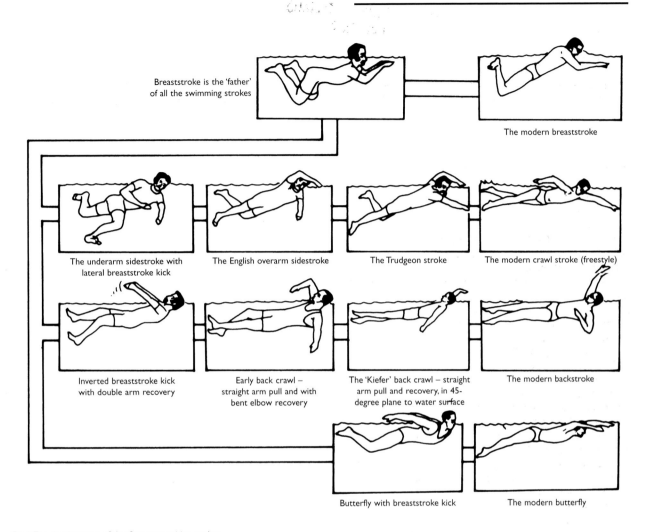

Breaststroke is the 'father' of all the swimming strokes

The modern breaststroke

The underarm sidestroke with lateral breaststroke kick

The English overarm sidestroke

The Trudgeon stroke

The modern crawl stroke (freestyle)

Inverted breaststroke kick with double arm recovery

Early back crawl – straight arm pull and with bent elbow recovery

The 'Kiefer' back crawl – straight arm pull and recovery, in 45-degree plane to water surface

The modern backstroke

Butterfly with breaststroke kick

The modern butterfly

Fig 1 The development of the four competitive strokes.

arm and leg movements. In direct contrast to freestyle and backstroke, the arms and legs must move simultaneously and in the same plane. Often mistakenly referred to as simply circling the hands and feet, breaststroke is the slowest of the four strokes and is the most controversial in terms of competitive disqualifications. Common causes of disqualification are touching the wall with one hand during the turn, performing a butterfly kick on the turn, or bringing the hands past the hips when pulling.

Butterfly is arguably the most spectacular swimming style. The swimmer's body undulates in a way that resembles the movements of a dolphin. The legs move simultaneously, with the arms arcing low over the water on the recovery, while the momentum of the whole body is used to propel the athlete forward. Common causes for disqualification are touching the wall with one hand during the turn, or using alternating motions of the arms or legs.

In Individual Medley events, the swimmer competes in every swimming stroke at equal distances. This event combines technique, speed and endurance, and is the aquatic equivalent of the Decathlon or Heptathlon in athletics. The sequence of strokes is as follows: butterfly, backstroke, breaststroke, freestyle.

Four swimmers from the same team compete in the Relay events. For the Freestyle Relay, all swimmers use this fastest stroke (although, technically speaking, any stroke would comply with the rules). Medley Relays use all four strokes, with the following sequence: backstroke, breaststroke, butterfly, freestyle. Backstroke is the first stroke because it allows the swimmers to start in the water and then change strokes safely with dive starts thereafter. Relay changeovers are valid when the feet of the outgoing swimmer detach from the blocks at least 3/100 of a second after the fingers of the incoming swimmer touch

Fig 2 Freestyle.
© *Steve Lindridge iDEAL iMAGES (Scotland)*

the wall. If the outgoing swimmer moves too early, his or her team is disqualified.

The Rules

The rules as presented here are correct at the time of going to print. The international governing body for swimming, the Fédération Internationale de Natation Amateur (FINA), reviews the rules on a quadrennial basis, with these rules being current until 2009.

SW 4 The Start
SW 4.1 The start in Freestyle, Breaststroke, Butterfly and Individual Medley races shall be with a dive. On the long whistle from the referee the swimmers shall step onto the starting platform and remain there. On the starter's command 'take your marks', they shall immediately take up a starting position with at least one foot at the front of the starting platforms. The position of the hands is not relevant. When all

swimmers are stationary, the starter shall give the starting signal.
SW 4.2 The start in Backstroke and Medley Relay races shall be from the water. At the referee's first long whistle, the swimmers shall immediately enter the water. At the Referee's second long whistle the swimmers shall return without undue delay to the starting position (**SW 6.1**). When all swimmers have assumed their starting positions, the starter shall give the command 'take your marks'. When all swimmers are stationary, the starter shall give the starting signal.
SW 4.3 In Olympic Games, World Championships and other FINA events the command 'Take your marks' shall be in English and the start shall be by multiple loudspeakers, mounted one at each starting platform.
SW 4.4 Any swimmer starting before the starting signal has been given, shall be disqualified. If the starting signal sounds before the disqualification is declared, the

race shall continue and the swimmer or swimmers shall be disqualified upon completion of the race. If the disqualification is declared before the starting signal, the signal shall not be given, but the remaining swimmers shall be called back and start again.

SW 5 Freestyle
SW 5.1 Freestyle means that in an event so designated the swimmer may swim any style, except that in Individual Medley or Medley Relay events, freestyle means any style other than backstroke, breaststroke or butterfly.
SW 5.2 Some part of the swimmer must touch the wall upon completion of each length and at the finish.
SW 5.3 Some part of the swimmer must break the surface of the water throughout the race, except it shall be permissible for the swimmer to be completely submerged during the turn and for a distance of not more than 15 metres after the start and each turn. By that point, the head must have broken the surface.

SW 6 Backstroke

SW 6.1 Prior to the starting signal, the swimmers shall line up in the water facing the starting end, with both hands holding the starting grips. Standing in or on the gutter or bending the toes over the lip of the gutter is prohibited.

SW 6.2 At the signal for starting and after turning the swimmer shall push off and swim upon his back throughout the race except when executing a turn as set forth in **SW 6.4**. The normal position on the back can include a roll movement of the body up to, but not including 90 degrees from horizontal. The position of the head is not relevant.

SW 6.3 Some part of the swimmer must break the surface of the water throughout the race. It is permissible for the swimmer to be completely submerged during the turn, at the finish and for a distance of not more than 15 metres after the start and each turn. By that point the head must have broken the surface.

SW 6.4 When executing the turn there must be a touch of the wall with some part of the swimmer's body. During the turn the shoulders may be turned over the vertical to the breast after which a continuous single arm pull or a continuous simultaneous double arm pull may be used to initiate the turn. The swimmer must have returned to the position on the back upon leaving the wall.

SW 6.5 Upon the finish of the race the swimmer must touch the wall while on the back.

SW 7 Breaststroke

SW 7.1 From the beginning of the first arm stroke after the start and after each turn, the body shall be kept on the breast. It is not permitted to roll onto the back at any time. Throughout the race the stroke cycle must be one arm stroke and one leg kick in that order.

SW 7.2 All movements of the arms shall be simultaneous and in the same horizontal plane without alternating movement.

SW 7.3 The hands shall be pushed forward together from the breast on, under, or over the water. The elbows shall be under water except for the final stroke before the turn, during the turn and for the final stroke at

Fig 3 Backstroke.
© Steve Lindridge iDEAL iMAGES (Scotland)

Fig 4 Breaststroke.
© Steve Lindridge iDEAL iMAGES (Scotland)

the finish. The hands shall be brought back on or under the surface of the water. The hands shall not be brought back beyond the hip line, except during the first stroke after the start and each turn.

SW 7.4 During each complete cycle, some part of the swimmer's head shall break the surface of the water. After the start and after each turn, the swimmer may take one arm stroke completely back to the legs. The head must break the surface of the water before the hands turn inward at the widest part of the second stroke. A single downward dolphin kick followed by a breaststroke kick is permitted while wholly submerged. Following which, all movements of the legs shall be simultaneous and in the same horizontal plane without alternating movement.

SW 7.5 The feet must be turned outwards during the propulsive part of the kick. A scissors, flutter or downward dolphin kick is not permitted except as in **SW 7.4**. Breaking the surface of the water with the feet is allowed unless followed by a downward dolphin kick.

SW 7.6 At each turn and at the finish of the race, the touch shall be made with both hands simultaneously at, above, or below the water level. The head may be submerged after the last arm pull prior to the touch, provided it breaks the surface of the water at some point during the last complete or incomplete cycle preceding the touch.

SW 8 Butterfly

SW 8.1 From the beginning of the first arm stroke after the start and each turn, the body shall be kept on the breast. Underwater kicking on the side is allowed. It is not permitted to roll onto the back at any time.

SW 8.2 Both arms shall be brought forward together over the water and brought backward simultaneously through-out the race, subject to **SW 8.5**.

SW 8.3 All up and down movements of the legs must be simultaneous. The legs or the feet need not be on the same level, but they shall not alternate in relation to each other. A breaststroke kicking movement is not permitted.

Fig 5 Butterfly.
© Steve Lindridge iDEAL iMAGES (Scotland)

SW 8.4 At each turn and at the finish of the race, the touch shall be made with both hands simultaneously, at, above or below the water surface.

SW 8.5 At the start and at turns, a swimmer is permitted one or more leg kicks and one arm pull under the water, which must bring him to the surface. It shall be permissible for a swimmer to be completely submerged for a distance of not more than 15 metres after the start and after each turn. By that point, the head must have broken the surface. The swimmer must remain on the surface until the next turn or finish.

SW 9 Medley Swimming

SW 9.1 In Individual Medley events, the swimmer covers the four swimming styles in the following order: butterfly, backstroke, breaststroke and freestyle.

SW 9.2 In Medley Relay events, swimmers will cover the four swimming styles in the following order: backstroke, breaststroke, butterfly and freestyle.

SW 9.3 Each section must be finished in accordance with the rule which applies to the style concerned.

SW 10 The Race

SW 10.1 A swimmer swimming over the course alone shall cover the whole distance to qualify.

SW 10.2 A swimmer must finish the race in the same lane in which he started.

SW 10.3 In all events, a swimmer when turning shall make physical contact with the end of the pool or course. The turn must be made from the wall, and it is not permitted to take a stride or step from the bottom of the pool.

SW 10.4 Standing on the bottom during Freestyle events or during the freestyle portion of Medley events shall not disqualify a swimmer, but he shall not walk.

SW 10.5 Pulling on the lane rope is not allowed.

SW 10.6 Obstructing another swimmer by swimming across another lane or otherwise interfering shall disqualify the offender. Should the foul be intentional, the referee shall report the matter to the Member promoting the race, and to the Member of the swimmer so offending.

SW 10.7 No swimmer shall be permitted to use or wear any device that may aid his speed, buoyancy or endurance during a competition (such as webbed gloves, flippers, fins, etc). Goggles may be worn.

SW 10.8 Any swimmer not entered in a race, who enters the water in which an event is being conducted before all swimmers therein have completed the race, shall be disqualified from his next scheduled race in the meet.

SW 10.9 There shall be four swimmers on each relay team.

SW 10.10 In relay events, the team of a swimmer whose feet lose touch with the starting platform before the preceding team-mate touches the wall shall be disqualified.

SW 10.11 Any relay team shall be disqualified from a race if a team member, other than the swimmer designated to swim that length, enters the water when the race is being conducted, before all swimmers of all teams have finished the race.

SW 10.12 The members of a relay team and their order of competing must be nominated before the race. Any relay team member may compete in a race only once. The composition of a relay team may be changed between the heats and finals of an event, provided that it is made up from the list of swimmers properly entered by a Member for that event. Failure to swim in the order listed will result in disqualification. Substitutions may be made only in the case of a documented medical emergency.

SW 10.13 Any swimmer having finished his race, or his distance in a relay event, must leave the pool as soon as possible without obstructing any other swimmer who has not yet finished his race. Otherwise the swimmer committing the fault, or his relay team, shall be disqualified.

SW 10.14 Should a foul endanger the chance of success of a swimmer, the referee shall have the power to allow him to compete in the next heat or, should the foul occur in a final event or in the last heat, he/she may order it to be re-swum.

SW 10.15 No pace-making shall be permitted, nor may any device be used or plan adopted which has that effect.

CHAPTER 2

GETTING STARTED –
FACILITIES AND EQUIPMENT

Facilities

Olympic champions have trained in pools of many different sizes, but the standard units of competitive swimming are short-course (25m) or long-course (50m) pools. Sometimes likened to the differences between indoor and outdoor athletics, performances in short- and long-course pools differ greatly from each other. Short-course pools are very common in the UK and are usually around six lanes wide (15m) and operated by local authorities. See Fig 6 for a short-course set-up. Races in short-course pools have more turns and therefore are faster by up to 2–3 seconds per 100m on some strokes.

Long-course pools are the standard size for the Olympic Games and must be ten lanes wide (25m) to accommodate international competition requirements.

Fig 6 A short-course set-up.

OPPOSITE PAGE: *Fig 7 A long-course pool.*

See Fig 7 for a long-course set-up at the National Swimming Academy in Stirling. There are only twenty long-course pools in the UK (just over half the number in the Australian city of Sydney, which has thirty-seven!), and only one of these (Sheffield) meets the international competition standard of being ten lanes wide. The lack of long-course facilities in Britain is often cited as a limiting factor in improving elite-level performance.

The sport of swimming across the world is based on a club structure. The system of a series of progressive squads is commonly used to develop performance. They are arranged according to age and ability and the limiting factor is usually the availability of sufficient time and space. The normal pool set-up for a squad training session in a six-lane × 25m pool is illustrated in Fig 8.

In terms of organization, alternate lanes swim in a clockwise and anti-clockwise direction for safety reasons, to avoid collisions. Swimmers are normally allocated to lanes according to speed. Some coaches may also assign lanes according to stroke specialisms.

Other essential facility requirements are the following:

- backstroke (turning) flags, set 5m from the wall so that swimmers can count their strokes before turns and finishes;
- lane lines (ropes), to divide the pool into lanes and organize groups;
- starting blocks (platforms), to practise competitive starts and relay changeovers; and
- pace (sweep) clocks, to time swims, rest intervals and spacing of swimmers.

Kit

It is essential that the correct equipment is used in developing a swimmer's ability. The main essentials are obvious – trunks or a swimsuit – but a variety of other 'gear' can be used to improve performance.

- Goggles: these are a must from the very beginning of swimming lessons, not only protecting the eyes from chemicals, but also helping swimmers to see techniques below the surface.

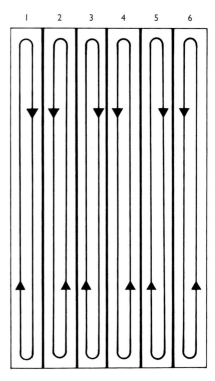

Alternate lanes clockwise and anticlockwise to avoid unnecessary collisions

ABOVE: *Fig 8 Pool layout and lane patterns.*

Fig 9 The swimmer's kit.

- Swim cap: in addition to the hygiene benefits, by keeping the hair from the eyes a swim cap can also help the swimmer to concentrate on developing stroke technique.
- Kickboard: these come in different shapes and sizes, but they are a staple of swimming programmes, to isolate and improve the leg action on breaststroke and frontcrawl. (Coaches tend not to use kickboards as often for butterfly or at all for backstroke.)
- Pull buoy: essentially a tool to isolate the arms, pull buoys come in different shapes and sizes. Some pull buoys are too large and buoyant for younger swimmers, resulting in the body position being unnaturally high compared with the position achieved when swimming the full stroke.
- Fins: short fins are harder to use, but very useful for technique and conditioning. Longer fins are better used in the early stages of development, although they can give a false sense of ability if over-used.
- Water bottle: to avoid dehydration in sessions lasting from 1–3 hours, swimmers should always have a water bottle filled with an appropriate drink.
- Rubber band: usually a makeshift band (25–50cm across) cut up from old tyre inner tubes, these simple bands can be an excellent technique and conditioning device when placed around the ankles, especially on backstroke.
- Tubing/stretchcords: used on land, tubing or a stretchcord can play a part in avoiding injury, for example, in warming up the rotator cuff muscles in the shoulder before training, or in training sessions to improve conditioning (perhaps in sets of 30 × double-arm fly reps in circuit training).

CHAPTER 3

THE AQUATICS FAMILY

The commonly used term 'swimming' actually refers to a number of aquatic disciplines governed by FINA. The discipline of competitive swimming is the most popular and has the highest media profile, but there are several other exciting activities in the aquatics family. There are Olympic competitions in Water Polo, Synchronized Swimming, and Diving. Open-Water Swimming is the newest and fastest-growing aquatic discipline and may appear in future Olympic programmes.

Water Polo

There is little documentation on the origins of water polo. However, we do know that the term 'polo' is the English pronunciation of the Indian word *pulu*, meaning 'ball'. Just as the ball game played on horseback became known as 'polo', so the ball game played in water became known as 'water polo', although there is no further connection between the two sports.

The game that evolved into modern water polo began as a form of rugby football played in rivers and lakes with the object being to 'carry' the ball to the opponent's side. By 1869, an Indian-rubber ball began replacing the original ball, which had been made from a pig's stomach. One year later, the London Swimming Club developed rules for a kind of football to be played in swimming pools. The first official game was played in the Crystal Palace Plunge in London.

Early games were generally exhibitions of brute strength. Passing, punting and dribbling were scarcely ever practised. Each player considered it his duty to score goals with little or no regard to position. A goal was scored by placing the ball, with two hands, on the top of the tank end. A favourite trick of the players was to place

the 5–9in (13–23cm) ball inside their swimming suit and dive under the murky water, then appear again as near the goal as possible. If the player came up too near the goal, he was promptly jumped on by the goalie, who was permitted to stand on the pool deck.

By 1880 in Scotland, the introduction of the Trudgeon stroke permitted rule changes to make the game faster. The game moved from a rugby style to a soccer style of play. The goal became a cage measuring 10ft by 3ft (3m by 1m) and a goal could be scored by throwing the ball into this area.

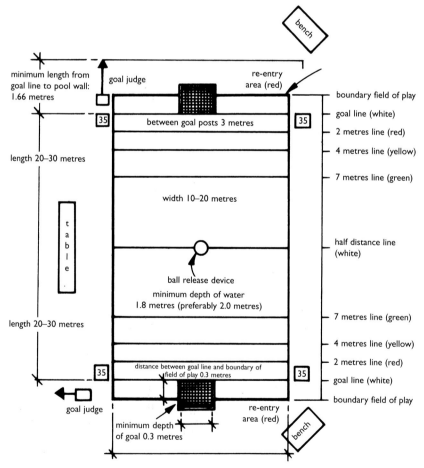

Fig 10 Pool layout for water polo matches.

The ball was also changed to a leather Association football (soccer ball). Players could only be tackled if they held the ball and players could only touch the ball with one hand at a time. In the late 1880s, these Scottish rules were generally adopted throughout Great Britain.

In 1888, the United States became the next country to play water polo when John Robinson, an English swimming instructor, organized a team at the Boston Athletic Association. The early American game was played in the 'old' English style, but soon developed its own, distinctly American characteristics. It involved close formations and fierce scrimmages and was one of the roughest games ever played. The ball would be taken underwater and held with two hands. Players grabbed each other where they chose, becoming locked in wrestling grips and losing interest in the whereabouts of the ball. It was a survival of the fittest. In many underwater battles, the strongest man would let go of the other only when he was no longer able to endure without air. Players often floated apparently lifeless to the surface or were pulled out of the water in need of resuscitation.

Water polo spread to Hungary in 1889, Belgium in 1890, Austria and Germany in 1894, and France in 1895. The sport was actually included in the Olympic Games of 1900 as an exhibition. Only club teams participated and Great Britain defeated Belgium, 7–2, in the final game. At the St Louis Games of 1904, the United States was the only country to participate. Germany showed an interest in entering, but declined after discovering that the American-style of water polo was to be played instead of the European or English–Scottish version of the game. In succeeding years, the British continued to dominate European and Olympic play, winning Olympic titles in London in1908, in Stockholm in 1912 and in Antwerp in 1920.

In 1911, a decisive advance was made in the game when FINA made the English–Scottish rules obligatory for all member nations. It is fair to say that it was not until the 1920 VII Olympiad in Antwerp, when twelve nations competed, that the game really became popular and internationally represented. Even then, the

Germans, Austrians and Hungarians were not permitted to participate due to their involvement in the First World War. From 1928, first Germany and then Hungary began a reign of dominance over international water polo, which lasted into the 1980s, when Yugoslavia, the United States, the USSR, Italy and Spain all fielded extremely competitive teams. The current Olympic champions are once again Hungary.

Women's water polo followed the same pattern of development as most of the rest of women's sport. It started with some interest in the early part of the 1900s and was then discontinued until after the Second World War. It was officially recognized as a World Championship sport in 1986 and as an Olympic sport in 2000 at Sydney. The current Olympic champions are Italy.

Synchronized Swimming

Synchronized swimming (usually shortened to 'synchro'), a sport often described as 'dance in the water', consists of special elements such as strength, flexibility, grace, artistry and long underwater endurance. In order for the athletes to stay longer underwater and perform routines, while at the same time appearing both presentable and comfortable, various 'methods' are used during a performance. One of them is a clip on the swimmer's nose, which prevents an intake of water through the nostrils, making it possible for the athlete to stay underwater longer; hair gel helps hair to stay in place and make-up highlights the athletes' features; underwater speakers transmit the music into the pool, helping the swimmers keep their synchronization while underwater.

Synchronized Swimming is one of only three Olympic disciplines in which only women are allowed to compete (the other two being Rhythmic Gymnastics and Softball). The pool where synchronized swimming takes place must be at least 3m deep over a 12 x 12m area in the centre of the pool. In Olympic Synchro, any country can enter in the duet and the

team event. Swimmers perform their routines in the water and are awarded two sets of marks, for technical merit and artistic impression.

The activity (as opposed to the competition) of synchronized swimming is almost 100 years old. In 1907, the Australian Annette Kellerman, performing in a glass tank, attracted attention in the USA at the New York Hippodrome as the first underwater ballerina. In 1915, Katherine Curtis, a student at the University of Wisconsin, experimented with diving actions and stunts in the water, and later set up a 'water ballet club' at the University of Chicago in 1923. The most famous synchronized swimmer of all time is probably Esther Williams (USA). Formerly an American Freestyle champion and Olympic contender, she popularized 'water ballet' with her performances in the San Francisco World's Fair Aquacade and subsequent MGM movies.

Organized Synchro competition began in the 1940s when the sport was recognized by the governing body of American Collegiate sport, the AAU. Internationally, the first 'demonstration' event took place at the 1951 Pan American Games in Buenos Aires, Argentina. Less than three years later, when FINA was formed, Synchronized Swimming became a division of aquatics and international competition was formally launched. Demonstration events were held at every Olympic Games, from Melbourne in 1956 to Moscow in 1980, but it was not until the Los Angeles Games of 1984 that Synchronized Swimming awarded its first official Olympic medals.

The leading nations in Synchro competition were initially the USA and Canada and their excellence continues to the present day. In recent years, as the sport's popularity has grown, their dominance has been challenged by Japan, Russia and France. Often under threat from administrators who criticize the sport's 'subjective' judging and artistic format, synchro has also been ridiculed in the media, and portrayed unfairly. Increasing numbers of men are involved in synchro swimming, although they are still by no means commonplace; one of the notables is American international Bill May.

Diving

The history of competitive diving spans roughly 100 years and during this period of development the nature of the activity has changed dramatically. Junior divers now routinely perform dives that were once banned at the Olympic Games because they were considered to be too dangerous. A report following the 1908 Olympics proposed a ban on the double somersault, because it was believed that a diver could not control the execution without risk of injury. Today, at the World Masters Championships, women in the 50–59 age group springboard competition are currently required to do eight dives – the same number as the women athletes in the Olympics of 1948.

Diving originated from people amusing themselves by jumping and diving from natural features (rocks and cliffs) or from structures built for other purposes (piers and bridges). In particular, travellers reported amazing feats performed by natives diving from the cliffs in Acapulco, Mexico, and in Hawaii.

In the early nineteenth century, the only 'dive' was a simple plunge, similar to that used by swimmers. The diver springs from the bathside and aims to travel as far as possible underwater. National Plunging Championships were held in Britain from 1883 to 1937 and continue to this day in Yorkshire.

The early competitions involved plain dives from platforms, the dive now referred to as a 'Forward Dive Straight'. While the Swedes performed graceful swallow dives, in Britain the dive was originally performed with the arms held above the head in flight, and was known as the 'English Plain Header'. However, this proved more difficult and less visually pleasing than the Swedish version, and eventually died out.

The sport as it is known today developed from gymnastics rather than from swimming. At the beginning of the twentieth century, the divers were mostly Swedish and German gymnasts who preferred to practise by landing in water, rather than on a hard floor. In summer, gymnastic equipment was transferred to the beaches so that gymnasts could perform acrobatics and land in the sea. Diving involving gymnastic movements such as somersaults and/or twists was referred to as 'fancy diving'. For some years, separate competitions were held for plain and fancy diving.

In Europe, fancy diving originated from platforms, and progressed to springboards. In America, diving started later and evolved from springboard diving. In Europe, the early platforms were temporary structures erected outdoors for the summer and then dismantled; most involved vertical ladders and were somewhat hazardous, particularly in windy weather. The early springboards consisted of planks of wood, covered in coconut matting to prevent divers from slipping. They were not very springy! In the early days there was no 'standard' springboard, so visiting divers having to use an unfamiliar board were always at a disadvantage.

In the early 1920s, most fancy dives from platform and springboard were performed in the straight position. As dives became more complex, the straight position became less feasible, as the rotation was too slow. In 1921 the Amateur Diving Association in England stated: 'Certain somersaults may be made with a bend at the hips and knees if the board is not sufficiently high to allow the limbs to be kept straight. "Back Front" dives should be performed with no bend at the hips or knees, but from a low board it will be found necessary to bend at the hips.' With the introduction of multiple somersaults, it became necessary to introduce the piked and tucked positions. In the 1920 Olympic Games, the Header Forward (straight), the Pike Dive and the Hunch Dive (tucked) were listed as three distinct dives. Later, it was decided to count them all as the same dive.

Diving developed rapidly through the first half of the twentieth century, with male divers first competing in the Olympic Games in 1904. For many decades the Games were dominated by Americans, but in recent years the Chinese have taken over. The 1928 Olympic competition included compulsory and voluntary dives; the compulsory dives were selected after each Olympic Games and remained in place for the following four years. This form of competition continued for twenty years. From 1949 to 1956 all dives were voluntary on platform and springboard, so the basic dives were rarely seen in competition. The conditions were then revised to include five required basic dives from the springboard, and restrictions on women's diving were removed.

In recent years, competitions in synchronized diving have been introduced and great advances in complexity have been achieved. This has largely been due to improved facilities and technology for training, such as trampolines with rigs, and high-speed cameras for the analysis of practice and competition efforts, as well as 'bubble machines' to break the water surface tension.

Open-Water Swimming

According to the ASA, Captain Webb, Lord Byron and others were the pioneers of open-water swimming. In 1875, Captain Webb achieved the crossing of the English Channel, considered today as one of the three toughest marathon swims in the world. Open-water swimming was officially recognized by FINA, the world governing body of swimming, in 1986, but it is possible to go back to the 1896 Olympic Games and realize that open-water swimming was the forerunner of today's indoor competitive swimming.

Lakes, rivers, canals and the sea all constitute 'open water'. 'Long-distance' open-water swimming is any swimming competition in open water over a distance of up to 25km. Events longer than this are referred to as 'marathon swims'. Pool events such as swimathons do not count. The British associations run competitions in Britain, and the ASA has run an Open-Water National Championship in England for 100 years. Formerly over 5 miles, the event has been brought into line with world events and is now over a distance of

5km. There is also a 25km long-distance event. FINA, the world governing body, has run a World Championship since 1986 and now its open-water events are incorporated into many major championships. It is also important to recognize the important work that the British Long Distance Swimming Association (BLDSA) has contributed to the sport. They have consistently encouraged the development of the sport by organizing a comprehensive review programme of competitions through the British summer. The Channel Swimming Association (CSA) and the Channel Swimming and Piloting Federation (CS&PF) regulate all swims in the English Channel.

There are a number of issues to remember when swimming in open water:

- there are no lines on the bottom. Swimmers need to look for landmarks to aid navigation, but they must find the balance between looking too often and not looking enough;
- when swimming in a warmer climate, apply plenty of sunscreen, not forgetting the lips;
- drink plenty of fluids before beginning;
- follow the buddy system. When swimming off a guarded beach, it is important to make the lifeguards aware of your plans.

Swimmers can do any type of training for open water – long straight swims, intervals where the intensity level is varied, even short sprints then treading or floating in place. It will be easier to count strokes compared to doing efforts for time or distance – 50 strokes at a high effort, 50 strokes easy, and so on. Base your training on time spent swimming, not how far you think you have gone. Stay on the safe side of distance from shore; do not go out too far. If you are in a race, watch out for the flailing arms and legs of those around you – getting hit or scratched hurts, and can knock off your goggles. Time your stroke so you can breathe without getting splashed in the face.

If you choose to swim in the open water, perhaps to add variety to your training, to practise for a triathlon, or to get ready for an open-water race, have fun and enjoy the freedom of swimming without walls.

Masters Swimming

Masters Swimming is an organized programme of swimming for adults, with the same administrative structure as for the other disciplines in the aquatics family. Members participate in a variety of ways, ranging from lap swimming for fitness to training for international competition. Anyone aged 18 or over can join Masters Swimming. In Britain, there are well over 400 Masters Swim Clubs (with more forming every year), with over 5,000 registered members, a few of whom are in their 90s! Everyone has their own reason for taking part – health, fitness, camaraderie, fun, the thrill of competition, travel and coaching are just a few.

For serious competitors, there are a large number of opportunities to test their skills and conditioning, both short- and long-course, at home and abroad. A recent Masters Swimming meet in the USA drew 2,400 participants, making it the largest swimming meet ever held in North America, while an international Masters championship in Japan has been recorded as the largest swimming meet ever. However, if competing is not your style, there is no need to feel pressured. Fewer than a third of Masters Swimmers compete in swimming meets on a regular basis – many are simply interested in the regular routine of working out and staying fit.

One of the greatest benefits of Masters Swimming is the opportunity it offers to practise with an organized group. Each club or team has its own programme. Some are highly structured, with set sessions and on-deck coaching, while others are very informal. However, the motivation and instruction a coach provides is a powerful advantage. Research has shown that interval training, an approach favoured by most coaches, has innumerable benefits over simple lap swimming, so most Masters Swimmers prefer structured sessions.

Competitions are organized by age groups of five-year increments (19–24, 25–29, 30–34, 35–39, and so on, to 95 and over). Events include 50, 100, 200, 500, 1,000 and 1,650 Freestyle (400, 800 and 1,500 in metres), 50, 100 and 200 Backstroke, Breaststroke and Butterfly, and 100, 200 and 400 Individual Medleys. There are also Freestyle and Medley Relays for men, women and/or mixed teams.

It is true that the thrill of competition can produce some anxiety in the form of 'butterflies', but study after study has proven that regular exercise can make a significant contribution to general health. Swimming has continually been identified as the best way to exercise. Stress reduction, weight control, cardiovascular fitness, reduced cholesterol, muscle tone and endurance are all positively influenced by exercise. Masters Swimmers swear by it.

Triathlon

Although it is not strictly speaking a discipline of FINA, there are strong connections between triathlon, one of the newest international sports, and swimming. Triathlon was invented in the early 1970s by the San Diego Track Club, as an alternative workout to the rigours of track training. The club's first event consisted of a 10km run, an 8km cycle and a 500m swim. In 1989, the International Triathlon Union (ITU) was founded, in Avignon in France, and the first official World Championships were held. The official distances for triathlon were set: a 1.5km swim, a 40km cycle and a 10km run, in that order. This standard distance, now called 'Olympic Distance', is used for the ITU World Cup series and the Olympic Games.

In 1994, at the IOC Congress in the French capital of Paris, triathlon was awarded full medal status on the Olympic programme and made its debut at the 2000 Sydney Games. Several high-profile 'pool' swimmers have switched codes to become triathletes and the ITU now has over 100 affiliated national federations around the world.

CHAPTER 4

EFFECTIVE TEACHING AND COACHING

Communication

Effective communication is fundamental to all forms of instruction, and an important aspect of leadership behaviour that all teachers and coaches should strive to improve. Initially, swimming teachers and coaches should attempt to master the following basics:

- correct positioning;
- projection of voice;
- using short, clear verbal instructions;
- using appropriate visual images.

However, these are no more than the absolute basics and ensure only that the swimmer will receive the appropriate instructions. In order to become effective communicators, swimming teachers and coaches also need to develop their communication skills and extend their range of communication possibilities. This will include mastery of a range of verbal, visual and manual forms of communication and an acceptance that not all information needs to come directly from them. The range of information that swimmers need includes organizational information, task and technical information and knowledge about their performance. The importance of effective communication in the swimming pool environment is even more significant when factors such as the acoustics of a large, noisy space, and water in the swimmers' eyes and ears are considered. Swimmers can rarely see or hear any feedback, which increases the communication challenges facing the swimming teacher/coach.

The practical limitations of the pool environment mean that there are few opportunities for pupils to come on to the poolside for interaction with the teacher/coach. Teachers and pupils thus operate in 'different' areas throughout most of the session, which limits both small-group and, particularly, individual interaction between them. At the average 25m pool, there is almost 80m of 'poolside' where teacher and pupil may or may not meet; the opportunities for individual feedback or exchange of ideas/information are very limited.

Best practice in modern educational thinking recognizes that, in order for teaching to be effective and for maximum learning to occur, the learner must 'participate' in the process. Therefore, teachers should do the following:

- observe the pupil/group to whom they are speaking and gauge their reactions during demonstrations or when setting tasks;
- involve pupils in responding to the information, by using a question and answer style;
- involve pupils in practical tasks that require provision of information, reasoning, decision-making, action and evaluation.

In the early stages of learning skills, a great deal of emphasis is often put on the teacher communicating with the swimmer about the performance. However, as the nature of the swimming environment and the teaching context do not facilitate extensive communication between one teacher and a large number of learners, it is more often desirable that more emphasis should be put on communicating with learners regarding other sources of information available about their performance, for example, peer support, self-review and so on.

Mastery of communication is obviously the basis of effective teaching and includes many aspects that expand on the basics. However, even the most effective communicator will be challenged if faced for 30 minutes with up to twenty pupils of varied ability in a crowded, noisy pool. Consider the average primary-school swimming class: from the usual average 30 minutes' allocation of water time, at least 10–15 minutes will be devoted to organizational matters and general instructions, leaving, at most, 10–15 minutes for the lesson. This is the time when the teacher could be observing, assessing and giving feedback to individuals or small groups. Research on teaching behaviour in swimming shows that 21.6 per cent of time is spent on management. Of the time spent on teaching, 43.1 per cent is spent on class instruction and 35.3 per cent on group instruction. This leaves only 21.6 per cent of time for individual instruction and feedback – not very much in the average lesson. If you doubt the amount of time that is spent on management, get someone to run a stopwatch during your lesson and see how long it takes to cover organizational matters, setting practices and class correction.

The amount of individual attention that can be devoted to any pupil is therefore very limited. As a result, the majority of a pupil's repetitions of a practice will often be done without supplementary information, or individual feedback on how they are performing. Staying on a practice long enough for one teacher to give a lot of individual feedback on performance will make the pace of a lesson very slow; the work will be very repetitive and pupils will probably become bored.

Watching pupils learning to swim, or working on improving technique, it is

OPPOSITE PAGE:
Fig 11 A coach at poolside.

obvious that those who are involved mentally as well as physically make far greater progress. Faster advances are made by those who are motivated to improve through appropriate objectives or targets and who work with meaningful instructions that they understand and can put into practice. Others who act without direction, for example, merely thrashing their way through the water without knowing what they should be doing, or without thinking about the technical points that are relevant, make much more limited progress. Repetition of the same faults clearly establishes those faults more firmly. Even where some progress is perceived over time, it is often due to physical development allied to age, or due to the physical effects of participation. Progress in such cases will

by no means be optimal. This is particularly true when the participant has acquired the basics of the skill or stroke; the next stage is the development of the technique, when greater refinement and control should be sought.

From observation of pupils' responses to the instructions given by the teacher, it is also clear that an individual pupil's interpretation and performance of the task set does not necessarily accurately match the instruction given. Often, due to a lack of awareness of what they are actually doing physically, performance is not closely related to what has been requested. Limited awareness of the position of the limbs leaves pupils thinking they are performing as directed, when in fact they are far from the movement

pattern required. Pupils therefore need either some way of knowing themselves what they are doing or an onlooker to let them know if they are doing the task correctly or what to change.

The adoption of different teaching styles or strategies for the presentation and practice of content offers opportunities to widen significantly the range of experiences that pupils have. Such experiences increase the knowledge and understanding that pupils have and that they can bring to their own practical performance. Some of these techniques can also significantly increase the amount of feedback that pupils can get on their own performance.

Teaching styles or strategies may be differentiated essentially in relation to who

Fig 12 Getting the message across.

makes the decision before (planning), during (carrying out) and after (evaluating) the lesson. The current trend is that in most teaching situations the teacher retains control of major decision-making of a planning nature and all decision-making of a safety nature but gradually encourages the pupils to do an increasing amount of the decision-making during the lesson. This can include decisions relating to the technical efficiency of strokes/skills. The objectives of such a process include making pupils more independent in their learning and making them more totally involved, that is, thinking as well as doing. The process also helps them to acquire other skills such as observation skills and appreciation of the performance of others.

In conclusion, the basics of communication are essential and are part of the fundamentals that we all must develop, maintain and enhance. Once developed, the ongoing development of these abilities throughout the span of the teachers'/coaches' career is also important. Greater appreciation of the problems of the learner and an appreciation of the complexity of the swimming teaching environment and context will help to encourage good practice in communication. In addition it is important to understand that communication does not have to come solely and directly from the teacher in order to be effective. Communication needs to be interpreted as something much wider than that and as something that utilizes a range of sources and forms. The important aspect is that it focuses on enabling learners to access any information, in a range of different forms and from a range of different sources, which will aid their performance. The teacher's role, in the class teaching situation, is not necessarily to communicate all information directly to every individual learner. Such a strategy is not logistically possible. The role is to make as much relevant information available in relation to the individual pupil's ability and the objective of the lesson. This needs to be in appropriate forms in order that they can process it and use it to maximize their performance.

Teacher and Coach Development

The Amateur Swimming Association (ASA) is the national governing body for Swimming, Diving, Water Polo and Synchronized Swimming in England. The Association also covers swimming for people with a disability, Aquafit, and Adult and Child activities. All ASA qualifications are recognized throughout Great Britain and in many other countries. Although there are separate governing bodies for swimming in Scotland, Wales and Ireland, the ASA is the major training organization for teachers and coaches for the aquatic disciplines across the UK.

The ASA offers qualifications covering a range of abilities and aspirations, from the Helper Certificate, which is aimed at those who wish to help their club or organization while under the guidance of a qualified ASA Level 2 Certificate for Teaching holder, to the Coach Certificate, which is aimed at those wishing to coach competitive swimmers operating at the highest level.

The full range of qualifications is shown in Fig 13.

The Swimmer Pathway

The infrastructure of swimming in Britain has been undergoing significant change in the past few years. Fig 14 illustrates a 'Swimmer Pathway', from learning to swim right up to elite level. This is also known as the Long-Term Athlete Development (LTAD) model.

LTAD is about achieving optimal training, competition and recovery throughout an athlete's career, particularly in relation to the important growth and development years of young people. Without a long-term approach to training there is likely to be a plateau in performance, when growth and development slow significantly, and for some swimmers this may result in worsening performances. At this point, the short-term training approach cannot be reversed. This often leads to drop-out before a swimmer has achieved close to their potential.

The ASA and Sport England state that there are five clear reasons for introducing a LTAD approach:

1 To establish a clear swimmer development pathway.
2 To identify gaps in the current swimmer development pathway.
3 To realign and integrate the programmes for developing swimmers and swimming in Britain.
4 To provide a planning tool, based on scientific research, for coaches and administrators.
5 To guide planning for optimal performance.

The following are some general observations on sporting systems from around the world (including Britain):

- young athletes under-train and over-compete;
- there are low training-to-competition ratios in the early years of development;
- adult competitions are superimposed on young athletes;
- adult training programmes are superimposed on young athletes;
- male programmes are superimposed on females;
- training in the early years focuses on outcomes (winning) rather than processes (optimal training);
- chronological age influences coaching rather than biological age;
- the 'critical' periods of accelerated adaptation are not fully utilized;
- poor training between 6–16 years of age cannot be fully corrected (athletes will never reach genetic potential);
- the best coaches are encouraged to work at elite level;
- coach education tends to skim the growth, development and maturation of young people;
- coaches, swimmers and parents, administrators and officials, all need to be educated in LTAD principles.

LTAD is a sports-development framework that is based on human growth and development. In short, it is about adopting

ASA ASSESSMENT PROCESS AND CERTIFICATION STRUCTURE

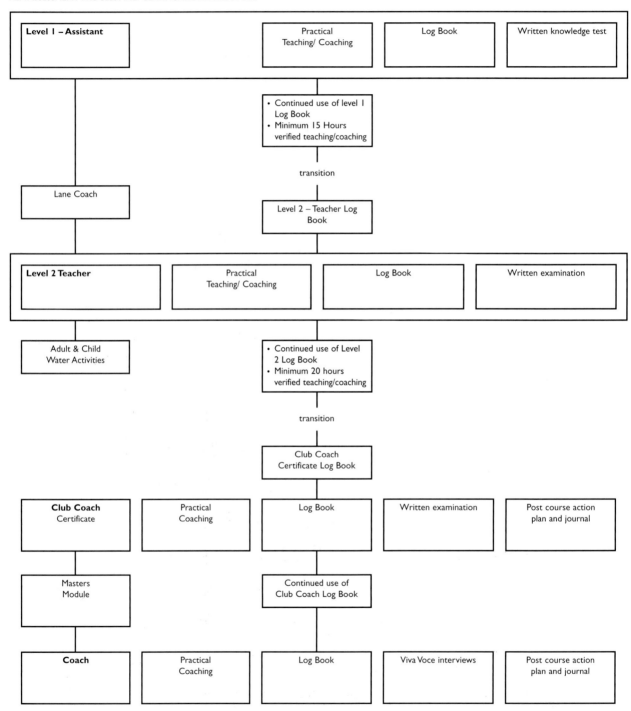

Fig 13 The ASA Assessment and Certification structure.

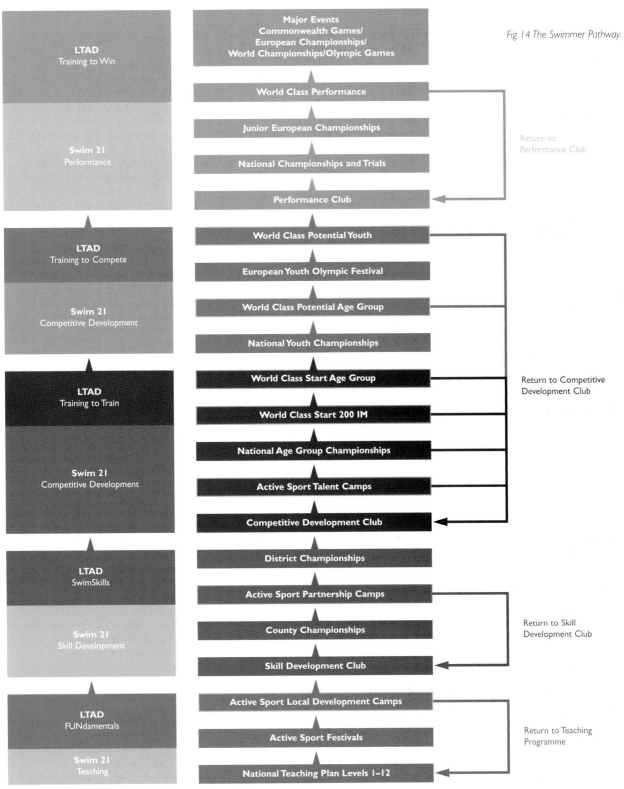

Fig 14 The Swimmer Pathway.

an athlete-centred approach to swimming development. All young people follow the same pattern of growth from infancy through adolescence, but there are significant individual differences in both the timing and magnitude of the changes that take place. Of course, human growth and development happen without training, but swimming training can enhance all of the changes. According to research, there are critical periods in the life of a young person when the effects of training can be maximized. This has led to the notion that young people should be exposed to specific types of training during periods of rapid growth and that the types of training should change with the patterns of growth. These have been used to devise a five-stage LTAD framework that has been been adapted to swimming:

KEY POINT

THE FIVE-STAGE LTAD FRAMEWORK:

Stage 1 – FUNdamentals:
              Basic Movement Literacy
Stage 2 – SwimSkills:
              Building Technique
Stage 3 – Training to Train:
              Building the Engine
Stage 4 – Training to Compete:
              Optimizing the Engine
Stage 5 – Training to Win:
              Top Performance!

Stage 1 – FUNdamentals

The FUNdamentals stage (girls 5 to 8 years; boys 6 to 9 years) should be structured and fun. The emphasis is on developing basic movement literacy and fundamental movement skills. The skills to be developed are the ABCs (Agility, Balance, Coordination, Speed), RJT (Running, Jumping, Throwing), KGBs (Kinesthetics, Gliding, Buoyancy, Striking with the body) and CKs (Catching, Kicking, Striking with an implement). In order to develop basic movement literacy successfully, participation in as many sports

as possible should be encouraged. Speed, power and endurance should be developed using FUN and games. In addition, children should be introduced to the simple rules and ethics of sports. No periodization should take place, but there should be well-structured programmes with proper progressions that are regularly monitored.

Stage 2 – SwimSkills

During this stage (girls 8 to 11 years; boys 9 to 12 years), young swimmers should be building technique, learning how to train and develop the skills of a specific sport. There may be participation in complementary sports, in other words, those sports that use similar energy systems and movement patterns. They should also learn the basic technical/tactical skills, and ancillary capacities.

KEY POINT

ANCILLARY CAPACITIES

- Warm up and cool down.
- Stretching.
- Hydration and nutrition.
- Recovery.
- Relaxation and focusing.

This stage coincides with peak motor co-ordination, so there should be an emphasis on skill development. Training should also include the use of 'own body-weight' exercises, medicine ball and Swiss ball exercises, as well as developing suppleness. Although the focus is on training, competition should be used to test and refine skills. The recommended training to competition ratio is 3:1. If a young swimmer misses this stage of development, he will never reach his full potential. One of the main reasons athletes plateau during the later stages of their careers is because of an over-emphasis on competition instead of optimizing training during this very important stage.

Stage 3 – Training to Train

During this stage (girls 11 to 14 years; boys 12 to 15 years), the aim is to 'build the engine', with an emphasis on aerobic conditioning. This is the stage at which there is greater individualization of fitness and technical training. The focus should still be on training rather than competition and the training should be predominantly of high-volume, low-intensity workloads. It is important to emphasize that high-volume, low-intensity training cannot be achieved in a limited time period, and therefore the time commitment to training should increase significantly. As the volume of training increases, there is likely to be a reduction in the number of competitions undertaken. However, there should now be specific targets for each competition undertaken, with a view to learning basic tactics and mental preparation.

During this stage, training should continue to develop suppleness and to include the use of 'own body-weight' exercises, medicine ball and Swiss ball exercises. However, towards the end of this stage, preparations should be made for the development of strength, which for girls occurs at the end of this stage and for boys at the beginning of the next stage. This should include learning correct weight-lifting techniques. The knowledge base of the ancillary capacities (how to warm up and warm down; how to stretch and when to stretch; how to optimize nutrition and hydration; mental preparation; regeneration; how and when to taper and peak; pre-competition, competition and post-competition routines) should be established.

Similar to the previous stage, if insufficient time is devoted to this stage or it is missed, then the young swimmer will never reach their full potential.

Stage 4 – Training to Compete

This stage (girls 14 to 16 years; boys 15 to 18 years) is about optimizing the engine. There should be a continued emphasis on physical conditioning with the focus on maintaining high-volume workloads, but

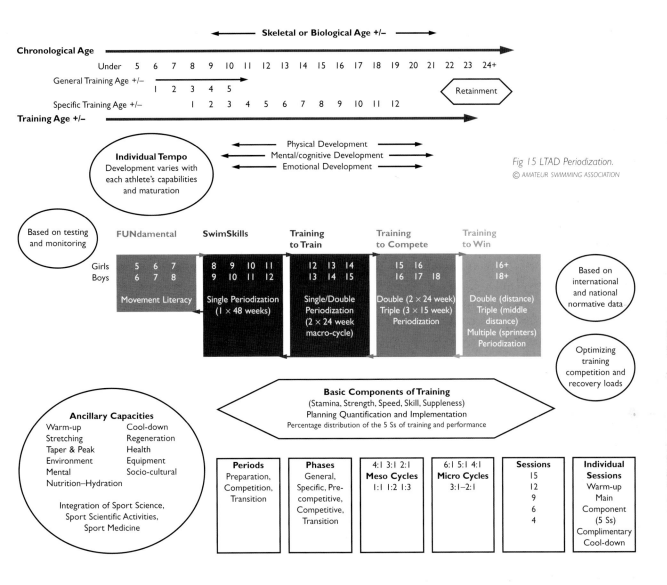

Fig 15 LTAD Periodization.
© AMATEUR SWIMMING ASSOCIATION

with increasing intensity. The number of competitions should be similar to the end of the previous stage, but the emphasis should be on developing individual strengths and weaknesses. This is done through modelling and nurturing technical and tactical skills based around specific strokes or distances, but not both. As a result, there should be either double or triple periodization of the training year. In addition, the ancillary capacities should be refined so they are more specific to the individual's needs. During this stage, training should also focus on developing maximum strength gain through the use of land training. This should be coupled with continued work on core-body strength and maintaining flexibility.

Stage 5 – Training To Win

This stage (females 16+ years, males 18+ years) is about top performance, and is the final stage of preparation. The emphasis should be on specialization and performance enhancement. All of the athlete's physical, technical, tactical, mental, and ancillary capacities should now be fully established with the focus shifting to the optimization of performance. Athletes should be trained to peak for specific competitions and major events. Therefore, all aspects of training should be individualized for specific events. There should be either double or triple periodization, depending on the events being trained for.

An illustration of the complexity of the LTAD process is shown in Fig 15 and explained in Chapter 15.

CHAPTER 5

SWIMMING FOR HEALTH

There is a strong connection between swimming for health and Masters Swimming (see page 21). Although the vast majority of Masters competitors are former swimmers, many members of Masters sections in swimming clubs are simply there to improve or to maintain basic fitness throughout their life.

Why Is Swimming Good for You?

Swimming is one of the few ways of getting exercise that improves your all-round fitness, because it can boost strength, stamina and suppleness all at the same time. It has all the cardiovascular benefits of running, with some of the strength-building effects of weight-training and some of the suppleness-promoting effects of a dance class. Swimming is a demanding aerobic exercise that helps to keep heart and lungs healthy. The extent to which particular groups of muscles are exercised in swimming will vary according to the stroke used, but a mixture of backstroke, freestyle and breaststroke will exercise all major muscle groups: abdominals, biceps and triceps, gluteals, hamstrings and quadriceps. Swimming also helps to keep joints flexible, especially in the neck, shoulders, hips and groin, as your limbs and body move through the water.

If you wish to lose weight, you can increase your level of physical activity by swimming and therefore increase the amount of energy you burn up – a vital component of a weight-management programme. Your GP or the staff at your local swimming pool may be able to help you in your aim to shed surplus pounds. A new ASA initiative called Swimfit also gives

Fig 16 Water competence means participating in a variety of aquatic activities.

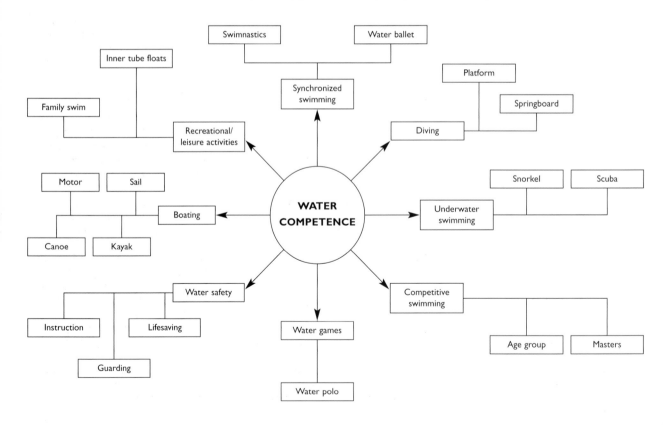

Fig 17 Swimming for health means swimming for life.

support and guidance to those who swim for fitness, including those who want to swim to lose weight.

Another benefit from the strength and improved co-ordination built up in swimming is the reduced risk of falls and hip fractures in the elderly. However, swimming will not build up your bones; weight-bearing land-based exercises do this.

Swimming is, generally, kinder to the body than land-based exercise because your natural buoyancy in water helps you avoid the jarring knocks that can cause injury. In water you weigh about a tenth of your normal weight, and the range of motion for the less fit person is much wider, as the water supports the weight of the limbs. Therefore, it is a good choice for people who want to exercise, but who might have problems with weight-bearing land-based activities. For example, swimming might suit those who have arthritis or back problems, weight problems or are pregnant. An added bonus for those with lung conditions, such as asthma, is that the air round a swimming pool is usually very humid, which makes breathing more comfortable.

Who Can Swim?

Swimming is an activity that is suitable for people of all ages and all levels of fitness, and is accessible to virtually everyone. From the unfit person taking their first few strokes in the shallow end, to the competitive swimmer training for a race, swimming is a physical activity that anyone can perform at their own level. Body shape will, however, determine how fast a person can swim for a given level of effort. So, while being able to swim faster is a marker of improving fitness, you should try not to worry about the speed of other swimmers around you. What is important is improving your own speed and swimming for a reasonable length of time.

Getting the Maximum Benefit

Of course, many people like to just splash around and enjoy themselves in 'leisure' pools with wave machines, waterfalls and slides. This does provide some physical activity, but at a low level. Those who want to gain the maximum health benefit from their time at the pool should decide on a more energetic programme. This could include walking the route to the swimming pool, or it could be combined with a few minutes on an exercise bike prior to getting in the water. If you are beginning a swimming-for-fitness programme and are lacking in fitness, start slowly, and progress steadily under the guidance of a qualified and experienced teacher or coach.

Swimming for 30 minutes a day, three to five times a week should give you a good amount of aerobic exercise to promote the health of the heart and lungs. However, it will have no effect on the strength of your bones. That is why it is a good idea to walk or jog or do other weight-bearing exercise alongside the swimming, because these help the bones to maintain or increase their mass. Of course you can incorporate other forms of exercise – water walking, water aerobics (sometimes called aquarobics), water yoga and stretching – in the water apart from swimming, either on your own or in classes. Your local pool will have details of sessions available.

PART 2
DEVELOPING YOUR TECHNIQUE

CHAPTER 6

FUNDAMENTALS

Swimming teachers and coaches frequently talk of 'fundamentals', but what do they mean by this term? Swimming is a repetitious and demanding sport. The skills involved are relatively simple when compared with a more complex activity such as gymnastics, but they must be done correctly all of the time if the swimmer is to be successful. In swimming, success lies in training the body to operate efficiently and effectively. Training with poor technique will put a swimmer at a disadvantage when racing against someone with better skills. A swimmer with good technique will be able to use energy more effectively than a swimmer who seems to be thrashing about in the lane.

Theories

There always has been, and still is, controversy surrounding the scientific explanation of the way propulsive forces are created in the four competitive strokes. The impact of types of resistance on swimming speed is not well understood, although, increasingly, it is noted as a limiting factor in the performance of elite swimmers. The clarification of these topics should produce better understanding and, hopefully, more effective coaching.

In the 1950s and 1960s, Americans James 'Doc' Counsilman and Charles 'Red' Silvia applied principles of conventional mechanics to the propulsive forces of competitive swimming strokes. In the early years, descriptions of swimming actions were based solely on observation of the movements of champion swimmers. Some credence was given to Newton's Third Law of Motion – 'To every action there is an equal and opposite reaction' – as being the theoretical basis for the propulsion involved. However, in the late 1960s, Counsilman offered the proposal that propulsion was gained through 'lift' rather than drag force. The basis of that theory was Bernoulli's Principle of Fluid Dynamics (see Fig 18), which is more commonly used to explain how aircraft fly.

In what appears now to have been a prophetic analysis, Silvia continued to interpret forces in competitive swimming strokes as being derived from Newtonian Laws, that is, when force is applied backwards, a swimmer will be propelled forwards. Recent analysis of stroke techniques using modern technologies has shown that proponents of the Bernoulli-Principle explanation were essentially flawed in their thinking. The previous research weaknesses of describing what happens when elite swimmers perform in training swims, and inferring those movement patterns to competitive performances plus restrictions to two-dimensional views of swimming, have been removed. In fact, it is only in breaststroke that lift forces exceed the importance of drag forces during propulsion.

Applying the Theory

Swimming educators and practitioners need to alter their thinking about the pulling patterns of the four strokes. The acceptance of Bernoullian lift as an 'explanation' for the major propulsion forces has led to a tolerance of large lateral, sweeping movements in pulling patterns. There is now conclusive evidence that such movements do not, in fact, maximize propulsive forces and are not demonstrated by today's best swimmers. This orientation will require a different approach to teaching and coaching from those popularly espoused.

Swimmers should not be taught or encouraged to produce exaggerated S-shaped, 'question-mark' or 'hourglass' (and so on) pulling actions. Such an approach will reduce propelling effectiveness, not enhance it. Swimmers should be taught or encouraged to 'feel' that they are pushing against the water in a predominantly backward direction. Promoting direct-action 'feel' and tolerating minimally necessary lateral movement components will go close

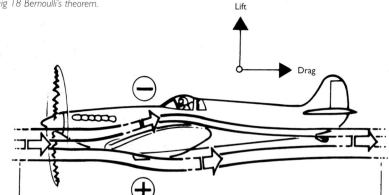

Fig 18 Bernoulli's theorem.

Lift

Drag

to maximizing propulsion and minimizing wasted energy and resistance. Lateral-movement components should occur naturally, whereas direct-force components should be emphasized. This does not imply that lift forces are not important or should not occur. The best propulsion will result from a stroke that has an optimal combination of both drag and lift-force components, such that their combined contribution to the forward direction is maximized for the energy expended. The role of the forearm as the major propelling surface should be stressed. This role increases as the speed of the swimmer increases. When swimmers are swimming as fast as possible, their attention should be on what the forearm is doing, with the hand being considered as an extension to this. Underwater footage of Australian swimming star Ian Thorpe provides the best example of the efficacy of this technique.

Newtonian Laws are more significant in relation to the actions observed in swimming. Bernoullian reasoning, on the other hand, is misleading and wrong, and inadequate to describe the complex phenomena of swimming. The actions of the arms in developing propulsive forces have to be balanced with the resistances that exist in the stroke. It would be inadvisable to increase resistance while increasing propulsive forces. Resistance increases much more rapidly than does speed. It is advocated that maintaining minimized resistance is of a greater priority than increasing propulsive force through extra effort or exaggerated movements.

For every technique change that is attempted in swimmers, its effect on drag has to be considered. If drag is increased, then it will most likely not be advantageous to change a swimmer's technique. An effective coach cannot ignore these components of resistance. If a swimmer attempts to go faster by producing more effort, and that effort alters technique to produce greater amounts of unproductive movements, then the added resistance caused by those movements may offset any potential speed benefits generated by the extra effort.

Fig 20 illustrates the importance of good streamlining in three of the four

strokes. The swimmers on the left-hand side are exhibiting a good body position. In the backstroke example, the swimmer on the right-hand side has the head held too high, causing resistance. In the breaststroke, the swimmer on the right has the knees coming too far forward, and in the butterfly example, driving the head too far underwater is causing resistance through greater undulation than is needed.

In order to swim fast, the technique must be efficient and produce the least resistance possible. Attention to drag factors will contribute to propelling efficiency and will make swimming fast much easier.

The relationship of increases in resistance to increases in speed creates a hierarchy of coaching preferences:

- Streamlining and the minimization of drag are paramount.
- Actions that cause vertical movements, particularly of the head, shoulders and hips, should be minimized and, where possible, eliminated.
- Actions that cause lateral movements, particularly of the head, shoulders and hips, should be eliminated.
- Technique alterations and actions should only be made when they do not upset the position and actions that minimize drag.
- Technique changes should not be made or modified if they produce a negative alteration in a swimmer's position and postural control in the water.

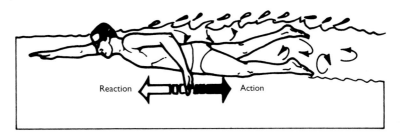

Fig 19 Newton's Third Law of Motion.

BACKSTROKE
a. good horizontal alignment
b. poor horizontal alignment

BREASTSTROKE
a. good horizontal alignment
b. poor horizontal alignment

BUTTERFLY
a. good horizontal alignment
b. poor horizontal alignment

Fig 20 The importance of good streamlining.

CHAPTER 7

THE BUILDING BLOCKS

Drills

Drills and technique work are an integral part of competitive swimming programmes across the world. Every coach and swimmer has a favourite drill or a 'special' technique, designed to enhance swimming performance. Drills also play a crucial role in assessing the current progress of stroke development by identifying both positive and negative elements of the swimmer's individual skill level.

Typically, drills are derived from observation of highly skilled swimmers. There is nothing wrong with this (it is always valuable to learn from an 'ideal model'); however, there are other considerations. First, there may be little value in using drills in isolation, without understanding their place in the overall learning process of the swimmer. This may even detract from the desired performance effects. Second, coaches must ask themselves whether the drill is suitable for the developmental level of the swimmer. Does the drill require muscular strength, swimming fitness,

zipper

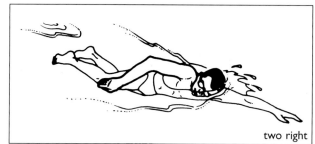
two right

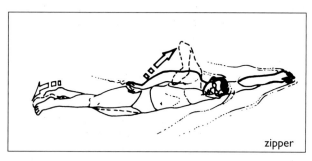
single arm backstroke

two left

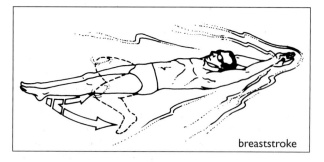
breaststroke

two full stroke butterfly

Fig 21 Examples of stroke development drills.

or a range of movement at a more advanced standard?

When using drills, coaches need to emphasize the key elements of control, precision, rhythm and co-ordination. To achieve the desired results, drills must be performed under close supervision, with appropriate feedback. Sloppy practice or less than total concentration on the drills will result in poor technique being reinforced. The old adage that '99 per cent right is 100 per cent wrong' is never more true than when practising stroke drills.

The generic term 'drill' is applied to countless variations of teaching techniques and coaching practices having a wide range of performance outcomes. It is helpful if this term is further broken down into four categories: stroke development; stroke correction; connecting drills; speed development.

Stroke Development Drills

'Practices designed to develop from the basics through to the whole stroke.'

These are the most commonly used drills and are an extension of basic learn-to-swim practices. The purpose of stroke development drills is to enhance the 'performance' of the swimmer. They are ideally practised prior to the main training set in a particular session, to review correct movement patterns and maximize the transfer of the stroke model into a 'performance' setting.

The concept of stroke development is generally expressed by a series of movement progressions, which build in their complexity, increase in their intensity, and maximize propulsive efficiency, while

minimizing overall resistance. Fig 21 gives examples of stroke development drills in each of the four strokes.

Variations on these drills involve the use of equipment and efficient application of propulsive force. For example, using hand paddles or fins can alter the level of sensory input, stimulating neuromuscular feedback so that stroke patterns are reinforced. However, these drills by themselves do not necessarily correct fundamental stroke faults when the whole stroke is swum. Stroke correction may require a more specific application of drills.

Stroke Correction Drills

'Practices that are designed to correct specific stroke faults.'

These drills work to correct a negative aspect of technique that is causing the swimmer to swim with decreased efficiency. These drills should not focus on cosmetic changes (which only make the swimmer look better), but should be applied to fundamental defects that limit the swimmer's performance potential. For example, a slight spread of the fingers is less important to the propulsive effect of freestyle arms than a major defect such as dropping the elbow during the middle of the stroke. The essential question to ask is: 'Will the stroke correction drill increase speed by improving efficiency?' If the answer is 'no', it should be left alone and the swimmer's efforts should be concentrated elsewhere.

Before introducing stroke correction drills, it is important to establish all the facts. Why is the swimmer's stroke not allowing for effective, fast swimming? Is the problem poor joint flexibility? Is it poor muscular strength? Is there a restriction because of injury? Is the swimmer limited by skill learning? Is the real problem motivational? And, above all else, what is the fundamental problem?

Designing stroke correction drills requires analytical skills from the coach, as well as an element of artistry. The coach must have a stroke 'model' to work from, but must also be aware of the individual

characteristics of the swimmer. Stroke correction drills can be utilized throughout a session, but care must be taken to ensure that fatigue does not become a limiting factor in performing the practices. A good analogy here is the repetitive practice of ballet dancers at the start of every day in front of the mirror. These practices reinforce correct technique and are done as precursors to more complex training. A coach may have a great variety of stroke development drills in his coaching repertoire, but his list of effective stroke correction drills is usually limited to a few for each stroke; they should always be determined by the specific requirements of each swimmer.

Drills in these first two categories must be linked to performance and often an intermediate step is required. The third category of drills is referred to as 'connecting drills'.

Connecting Drills

'Practices designed to link the performance of basic movements to the execution of the whole stroke sequence under competitive conditions.'

One of the great dilemmas of coaching is deciding when to make a stroke correction and when to concentrate on other training priorities. Certainly, when swimming technique is incorrectly applied, then the physiological benefits of training are not fully realized. However, if the continuity of training is always broken to redefine technique (in other words, to make a major stroke correction), then the effect of the training is reduced. There are times when it is not appropriate to stop swimmers, for the purpose of making a correction, during a main training set. Experienced coaches intuitively know when this is the case.

This does not mean that coaches should be dismissive of stroke correction during training. The coach should be constantly monitoring technique during training sets, but interaction with the swimmer usually takes the form of giving verbal or visual cues to help the swimmer re-focus attention, rather than specific drills to assist with this. If there is a need to repeatedly stop swimmers to correct technique during a main training set, it could be argued that the swimmer was not adequately prepared to undertake the training set in the first place. This is where drills have their greatest impact, as an adjunct to total stroke preparation and maintenance. Swimmers must be prepared to train using an efficient technique and must be able to use that technique under pressure situations. Connecting drills allow the coach to apply the elements of both reinforcement and correction to performance.

KEY POINT

Stroke drills are not 'easy swimming', but are about doing fewer strokes with a maximum of effort and concentration and eventually, under demanding pressure, lead to speed and perfection.

Connecting-drill sets should include the key elements of pace, stroke count and stroke rate, as well as the skill elements of the drill. These drill progressions usually serve a dual purpose as a physiological training stimulus as well as neuromuscular patterning. Because these drills have a performance component, the results over time will indicate the collective improvements in both fitness and stroke efficiency. In fact, some coaches even go so far as to suggest that these drills should be incorporated into certain test sets. Examples of connecting drills include variations of 'catch-up' freestyle (see Fig 22).

In addition to being used before main training sets or test sets, connecting drills can be used following a training set. In this case, the purpose is not to prepare the swimmer, but to reinforce a movement skill under fatigue conditions. Ultimately, the coach wants to achieve stroke technique that does not break down during competition when the swimmer experiences fatigue.

Speed-Development Drills

'Practices that are performed faster than race pace or focus on the stroke components of hand speed and acceleration.'

Speed-development drills highlight the interaction between the variables of stroke rate and stroke length at different swimming paces. The primary goal of these drills is to develop stroke efficiency at the speeds that are used during competition. Sometimes, paddles or fins are used in conjunction with speed drills. Because the speed of movement is the critical variable in these drills (unlike stroke-development drills, where paddles or fins are used for sensory input), the training outcome becomes muscular overload. Speed-development drills represent one way of translating strength gains achieved through land-based training into specific power gains in the water. However, there is a danger of over-use or excessive loading (especially if using very large paddles or fins) if the drills are prescribed indiscriminately.

Speed drills, with or without the use of training aids, are performed over short distances (usually no more than 25m) at a very high energy output; therefore, sufficient rest between repeats must be a consideration. These drills are best performed at the start of a training session, when the swimmer is fresh, placing the emphasis on the desired energy production. Examples include the backstroke 'bucket' drill.

Key Points on Drills

Many stroke-development drills rely on kicking to stabilize the body and provide propulsion. The drill progressions themselves can be an effective alternative to kicking with a kickboard. Using drills to strengthen and condition the legs has the added benefits of reinforcing a body position that is streamlined, and forces swimmers to co-ordinate their breathing.

Drills are given added value if the various aspects are taught in the following progression:

1 body position;
2 body position with kick;
3 feel of the arm stroke;
4 hand acceleration;
5 control of kick;
6 distance per stroke; and
7 stroke count.

A combination of all of the above is repeated at progressively faster speeds and under race pressure.

Observing young or less skilled swimmers usually reveals that their desire to swim faster is translated into faster arm and leg movements. One benefit of intelligently constructed drills is that young swimmers gain a better 'feel of the water' and understand that fast swimming is the result of the application of good swimming technique.

The value of drills does not diminish as a swimmer's career progresses. Coaches at the senior level should take the time,

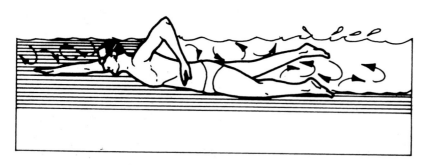

Fig 22 Standard 'catch-up' freestyle.

through one-on-one coaching contact, to 'fine-tune' a swimmer's stroke. Just as experienced concert pianists still practise their 'scales' every day, swimmers should ensure that their techniques are grooved to perfection. Precision and attention to detail, refinement and evaluation are all components of a long-term strategy for competitive stroke development.

The coach must also pay close attention to the precision of drill application. Because drills tend to focus attention on components of the total stroke, it is possible to target inherently weak points of the stroke pattern, such as the hand entry or exit. As with any movement, if the start is made correctly there is a better chance that the continuation of the movement will be correct. When evaluating the effectiveness of a drill, the coach must never overlook the integration of movements (for efficient propulsion) and positioning of all segments of the body (for reduction of resistance).

Sculling

Back in the 1970s, sculling was a central feature of swimming teaching. It is rather overlooked today, despite the fact that swimmers of all ages and stages can benefit from the improved 'feel for the water' developed by sculling practices. A fundamental element of synchronized swimming, sculling can be done with very large, or very precise movements. Some commonly used sculling practices in the development of the four strokes are illustrated in Figs 23–26, and there are many more.

These can be used as beginner practices for children just starting to swim or incorporated in the training and warm-up routines of Olympic champions.

> **KEY POINT**
>
> - A drill done 99 per cent right is 100 per cent wrong.
> - Drills are an effective tool for isolating the difference between propulsion and resistance; propulsive force without proper streamlining is wasted and great streamlining without propulsion is ineffective.
> - Successful swimmers do not train or practise with poor technique.
> - No drill is perfect. Select the one that will work best for you, and practise, practise, practise.
> - Teaching drills correctly is like teaching completely different strokes. If you have five key drills for each stroke, in effect you have twenty different strokes.
> - New drills should be taught near the beginning of a session when the swimmer's mind and body are most receptive to learning.
> - A learning and skill-development progression should be established.
> - Drills are about performing fewer strokes with precise effort and concentration in each stroke. Drills have nothing to do with easy or lazy swimming.

Fig 23a, b, c Fingers-down sculling.

OPPOSITE PAGE:
*Fig 24a, b, c
Midpoint sculling.*

THIS PAGE:
*Fig 25a, b
Extended sculling supine.*

Stroke Analysis

When observing swimmers in action, the teacher or coach needs to look at the whole technique to get an overall picture of efficiency. He should be looking for streamlining, smooth, unhurried actions and a co-ordinated rhythm. It is also helpful to analyse the stroke in a sequential manner, from the larger, gross movements to the finer, more precise elements of the technique. The following headings are intended as a guide to evaluating stroke technique in the four competitive strokes.

Body Position

The following should be checked:

- head position and line of vision;
- the relationship of the hips to the surface through the stroke;
- whether the body is horizontal throughout the full stroke cycle;

Fig 26a, b Extended sculling prone.

FRONT CRAWL

BODY POSITION

Flat ☐
Angled ☐
Rolling ☐
Sideways wiggle ☐
Head in line with body ☐
Head too high ☐
Head too low ☐
Hips high ☐
Hips low ☐

LEG ACTION

From hips ☐
From knees ☐
Deep ☐
Shallow ☐
Ankles flexible ☐
Ankles stiff ☐
Efficient ☐
Inefficient ☐

ARM ACTION

Entry
  Front of shoulder ☐
  Outside of shoulder ☐
  Across centreline ☐

Pull
  Straight arm ☐
  Bent arm ☐
  High elbow ☐
  Dropped elbow ☐
  Under body ☐
  Outside body ☐

Arms
  Strong ☐
  Weak ☐
  Inefficient ☐
  Continuous ☐

Recovery
  Bent arm ☐
  Elbow peaked ☐
  Direct ☐
  Wide sweep ☐

Shoulders
  Flexible ☐
  Stiff ☐

BACK CRAWL

BODY POSITION

Flat ☐
Angled ☐
Rolling ☐
Bobbing ☐
Head steady ☐
Head too high ☐
Hips high ☐
Hips low ☐

LEG ACTION

From hips ☐
From knees ☐
Deep ☐
Shallow ☐
Ankles flexible ☐
Ankles stiff ☐
Efficient ☐
Inefficient ☐

ARM ACTION

Entry
  Use time on clock e.g.
12 o'clock: five to one ☐

Pull
  Straight arm ☐
  Bent arm ☐
  'S' pull ☐
  Along body line ☐
  Under body ☐
  Continuous ☐

Release
  Link finger first ☐
  Thumb first ☐
  Back of hand first ☐

Recovery
  Straight over the body ☐
  Low, lateral movement ☐

BUTTERFLY

BODY POSITION

Flat ☐
Excessive undulation ☐
Hips high ☐
Hips low ☐

LEG ACTION

From hips ☐
From knees ☐
Deep ☐
Shallow ☐
Ankles flexible ☐
Ankles stiff ☐
Efficient ☐
Inefficient ☐

ARM ACTION

Entry
  In front of shoulder ☐
  Outside of shoulder ☐

Pull
  Bent arm ☐
  Elbows up ☐
  Keyhole ☐
  Continuous ☐

Arms
  Strong ☐
  Weak ☐
  Efficient ☐
  Inefficient ☐

Recovery
  Straight arm ☐
  Bent arm ☐
  High ☐
  Low ☐
  Clean ☐

BREASTSTROKE

BODY POSITION

Flat ☐
Angled ☐
Bobbing ☐
Shoulders horizontal ☐
Head too high ☐
Held out of the water ☐
Raised and lowered
for breathing ☐

LEG ACTION

Wide ☐
Narrow ☐
Simultaneous ☐
Screw kick ☐
Kick feet turned outwards ☐
Ankles flexible ☐
Ankles stiff ☐
Efficient ☐
Inefficient ☐
Whip kick ☐

ARM ACTION

Simultaneous ☐
Wide ☐
Narrow ☐
Straight arm ☐
Bent arm ☐
Beyond shoulder line ☐
Efficient ☐
Inefficient ☐
Continuous ☐

Recovery
  Elbows in ☐
  Elbows out ☐
  Palms up ☐
  Palms facing ☐
  Palms down ☐

Fig 27 A basic stroke analysis checklist.

- the extent and control of the longitudinal rotation in the long-axis strokes (freestyle and backstroke);
- the extent and control of the horizontal movement in the short-axis strokes (butterfly and breaststroke).

Leg Action

- See where the movements start and finish.
- Is the leg action for balance or propulsion?
- Look at the foot position throughout the whole movement.

Hands and Arms

- Look at the entry and catch.
- Where is the elbow in relation to the shoulders and hands?
- Watch the position and the pathway of the hands.
- Is the recovery smooth and controlled?

Breathing

- Watch to see if breathing is regular, at optimum frequency.
- Is the breathing action performed smoothly?

- Does the breathing affect other parts of the stroke?

Timing

- What is the relationship of each part of the stroke?
- Is there continuity in the full stroke cycle?

For an example of a checklist used in the early stages of the ASA certification programme, see Fig 27 on page 43 (with thanks to tutor Tony McKay for his permission to reproduce this checklist).

CHAPTER 8

BUTTERFLY

Background

Nicknamed 'the fly', the butterfly is the newest and most physically demanding of the strokes, but is also the most graceful to watch. The butterfly features the simultaneous overhead stroke of the arms combined with the dolphin kick, in which both legs move up and down together. Butterfly was developed in the 1930s and evolved from the breaststroke. However, it did not become an official Olympic stroke until the 1956 Melbourne Games. In 1934, David Armbruster, coach at the University of Iowa, devised a double over-arm recovery out of the water. This 'butterfly' arm action gave more speed but required greater training and conditioning. Controversy followed and, while not everyone was doing this quasi-breaststroke, those swimmers who did were winning races with good times.

In 1935, Jack Sieg, a University of Iowa swimmer, developed the skill of swimming on his side and beating his legs in unison like a fish's tail. He then adapted the leg action to be done face down. Armbruster and Sieg combined the butterfly arm action with this leg action and learned to co-ordinate the two efficiently. With two kicks to each butterfly arm action, this kick eventually became known as the dolphin fishtail kick.

Even though the butterfly breaststroke, as it was called, was faster than the breaststroke, the dolphin fishtail kick was declared a violation of competitive rules. For the next twenty years, champion breaststrokers used an out-of-water arm recovery (butterfly) with a shortened breaststroke kick. In the late 1950s, the butterfly stroke with the dolphin kick was legalized as a separate stroke for competition and the best swimmers today are almost as fast on 'the fly' as they are on freestyle.

Fig 28a Butterfly, side view.

Fig 28b Butterfly front view.

Contrary to popular belief, butterfly is not harder to do, harder to learn or harder to teach than the other strokes. The photographs and descriptions that follow are aimed at improving performance in butterfly to a competent level.

Technique

Body Position

The body should lie on the front in a horizontal position and there should be a continuous, rhythmic undulating movement. The hips should remain fairly close to the water surface and act as a central fulcrum in the movement. The head should be held centrally in line, with the face in the water and the eyes looking forward and down.

See Figs 29a and 29b.

Feet and Legs

The feet and legs should move in a simultaneous vertical motion. The knees should bend to bring the feet towards the surface, with the toes just breaking the surface.

The feet and toes should be long and pointed and extended from the ankle throughout. On the 'down kick'; the lower legs and feet thrust back and down against the water, driving the hips up and forwards. On the 'up kick', the knees should be pushed up with the legs straight, pushing the hips downwards.

See Figs 30a and 30b.

Hands and Arms

Entry

Hands should enter in front of the head, shoulder-width apart, with palms facing diagonally outwards. The hands should submerge before the elbows.

The hands should pause slightly as the body moves forward and should start to move down and out.

See Figs 31a and 31b.

Propulsion

The hands should scull outwards and downwards then press backwards (see Fig 32a). The elbows should remain high and point towards the side (see Fig 32b). The hands and arms should then sweep inwards, pressing towards and under the stomach, with thumbs nearly touching. The hands should then sweep outwards and backwards towards the legs (see Fig 33). This pulling pattern is commonly described as a 'keyhole' shape, but this is too simplistic and may misrepresent the actual mechanics of propulsion in the

Fig 29a, b Butterfly body position.

Fig 30a, b Butterfly feet and legs.

Fig 31a, b Butterfly entry.

stroke (see the explanations in the section on Fundamentals). Many swimmers are much more direct in applying force 'backwards', but the high, fixed elbow position remains crucial.

Recovery

The elbows should lead out of the water, still slightly bent. The hands should follow and once clear of the water should swing forward, above the surface with wrist and hands relaxed, back to the entry position (see Fig 34).

OPPOSITE PAGE:
TOP: *Fig 32a Butterfly catch.*

BOTTOM: *Fig 32b Butterfly pull.*

THIS PAGE:
RIGHT: *Fig 33 Butterfly exit.*

BELOW: *Fig 34 Butterfly recovery.*

Fig 35 Butterfly timing of second kick.

Breathing

The breath should be taken by raising the head to the front in a smooth movement, bringing the mouth clear of the surface. The chin should be pushed forward above the surface. The head should be lowered straight down, returning the face to the water, before the hands enter.

Timing

The legs should kick twice in each arm cycle. The first kick should occur just after the hands enter. The second kick should occur as the hands finish the propulsion phase (Fig 35). The breath should be taken at the end of the arm pull, as the legs are kicking. The face should be in the water, before the hands enter. A breath should be taken every one or two cycles.

Butterfly Start, Turn and Finish

Start

Control The swimmer should be able to demonstrate complete control at the front of the block, with no movement or rolling. A traditional 'grab start' controlled position is shown in Fig 36. The toes are curled over the edge and balance is maintained, with the hips as far forward as possible and the head tucked in.

Reaction The swimmer should have a fast response to the signal.

Signal to Entry The swimmer should thrust up and out from the starting block, achieving optimum height and distance.

Entry There should be a smooth entry, led by the hands, then with straight arms, the

head in line, followed by the hips and legs, with the feet making a limited splash.

Transition to Swim There should be a streamlined glide under the surface with the hands and head directing the body towards the surface. The feet should start kicking almost immediately. The arms should pull the body to the surface for transition to full stroke. The swimmer should not breathe during the first stroke cycle. The rules permit the swimmer to travel up to 15m underwater before starting to swim. Swimmers should be encouraged to take full advantage of this as they develop, according to age, skill and fitness.

Turn (Figs 37a–e)

Flag to Wall The stroke length should not change during the last 5m. The body

Fig 36 Grab start.

Fig 37a, b, c, d, e Butterfly turn and push-off.

Fig 38 Butterfly finish.

should be streamlined at the touch, with elbows slightly bent and there should be no extra glide. There should be a two-handed touch as per the laws.

On the Wall There should be a good tuck and pivot action with the head staying low. One arm should move over the water and the other below the water as both feet are placed on the wall, with the knees bent.

Push-Off The arms should be placed above the head, under the surface of the water, as the feet and legs push. There should be a streamlined glide under the surface, with the hands and head directing the body towards the surface.

Transition to Swim The feet should kick just before the body starts to slow down. Both arms should pull for a smooth transition into full stroke at the surface.

The swimmer should not breathe during the first stroke cycle.

Finish (Fig 38)

The stroke length should not change during the last 5m. The body should be streamlined at the touch, with elbows straight and no extra glide. The finish should be positively registered with a two-handed touch as per the laws.

CHAPTER 9

BACKSTROKE

Background

Backstroke is the second-slowest stroke after breaststroke. Due to the alternating arm stroke, there is always one arm engaged and the overall swimming speed does not vary very much throughout each stroke cycle. The maximum swimming speed is around 1.52m per second. Due to its position on the back, backstroke uses different muscles in the upper body from other strokes.

Backstroke was the first regulated style other than freestyle swum at competitions, and the 1900 Summer Olympics in Paris featured a 200m Backstroke race. In its early days, backstroke was swum with straight arms below the surface and bent arms above; today, it is the opposite! Rules for backstroke have changed significantly in the past twenty years, with first the restriction of 15m being placed on the distance allowed underwater after the starts and turns and, more recently, the introduction of a 'flip turn', done by rotating on to the front at the end of each length.

Technique

Body Position

The body should lie in a flat, streamlined position, with the head held perfectly steady in a central position. The shoulders and chest should be clear of the surface, with the hips and seat slightly submerged. There should be a controlled rolling of the shoulders round the long axis as each arm performs its alternating action. The ears should be close to water level and the eyes should look up and forward at about 45 degrees.

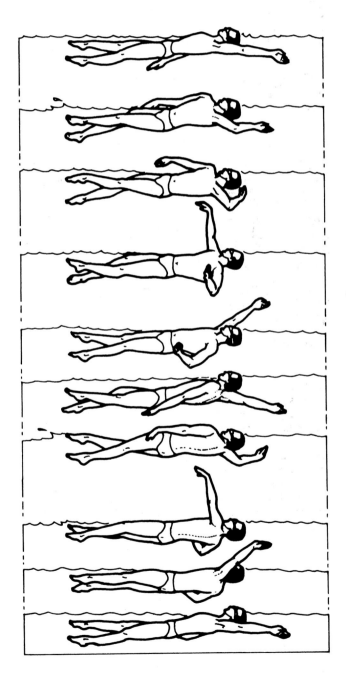

Fig 39a Backstroke, side view.

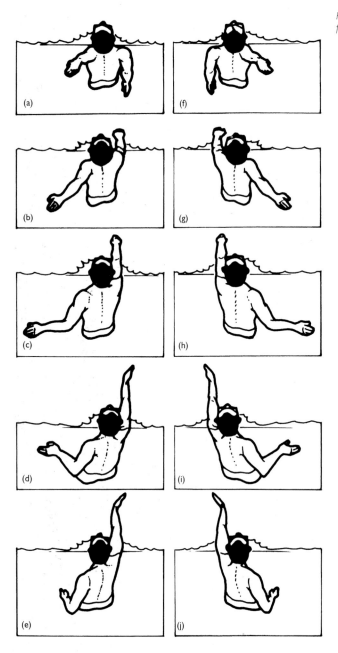

(a)
(b)
(c)
(d)
(e)
(f)
(g)
(h)
(i)
(j)

Fig 39b Backstroke, front view.

The 'up kick' should be initiated at the hips and finish with a strong positive thrust of the top of the foot and the lower leg. The 'down kick' should be more relaxed, with the knee starting straight, until in line with the body. The knee should then bend slightly, allowing the relaxed ankle to move to a deeper position, ready for the 'up kick' (see Fig 40b).

Hands and Arms

Entry (Fig 41)

The hand should be 'placed' in the water with elbow straight and wrist extended. The hand should enter directly ahead of the shoulder with the palm facing outwards allowing the little finger to enter first. The hand should continue downwards smoothly as the shoulders roll to that side.

Propulsion

The hand should exert force on the water, with the palm facing out and slightly down, away from the body (see Fig 42). The hand should then angle towards the feet as the elbow bends and points to the bottom of the pool (see Fig 43). The hand should sweep round, just below the surface of the water, before starting to angle down and inwards as it sweeps towards the pool floor. The elbow should straighten as the hand reaches its deepest point, just below the hips, just before a vigorous sweep inwards towards the leg and up towards the surface.

Recovery

The shoulder should lead the recovery, as it rolls up and round, as the hand leaves the water with the thumb directed upwards (see Fig 44). The elbow should be kept completely straight. The line of the recovery should be absolutely straight, above the shoulder to the entry point.

Feet and Legs

The feet and legs should maintain a steady, positive alternate kicking action. At the bottom of the kick, the knee should be slightly bent, with the foot long, pointed and slightly 'in-toed'. At the top of the kick, the knee should be straight, just below the water level, but with the toes breaking the surface. The legs should move alternately, passing close to each other in a continuous flutter-kick action (see Fig 40a).

Breathing

This should occur naturally in relation to the effort phases of the arm action. There should be a regular exchange of breath during each stroke cycle.

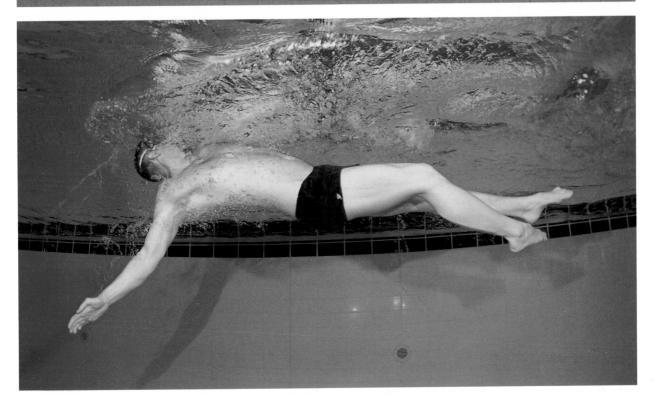

Fig 40a, b Backstroke kick.

OPPOSITE PAGE:
TOP: *Fig 41*
Backstroke entry.

BOTTOM: *Fig 42*
Backstroke catch.

THIS PAGE:
RIGHT: *Fig 43*
Backstroke pull.

BELOW: *Fig 44*
Backstroke exit.

Fig 45 Backstroke starting position.

Timing

There should be six beats (three of each leg) to each full arm cycle. One should be completing the propulsive phase as the other is ready to begin. Timing should be consistent and continuous with control.

Backstroke Start, Turn and Finish

Start

Control The swimmer should adopt a comfortable position on the wall, with legs, arms and head ready to respond to the starting signal (see Figs 45 and 46). The hands grip the bar outside shoulder width, one foot is slightly higher than the other and the body is held close to the wall, ready to uncoil powerfully on the starting signal.

Fig 46 Backstroke start, side view.

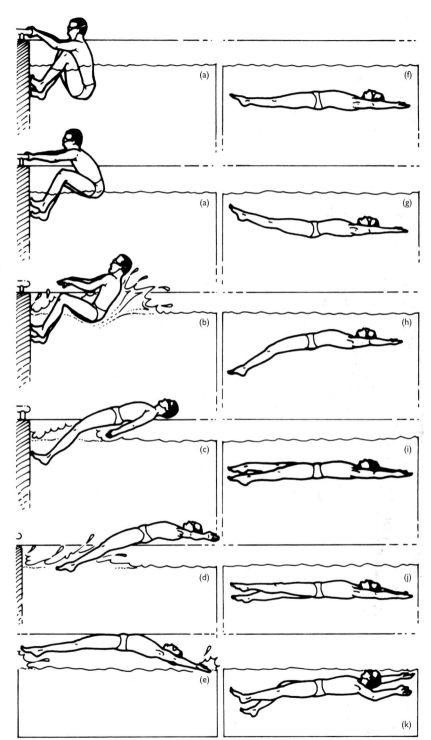

Reaction The swimmer should have a fast response to the signal.

Signal to Entry The swimmer should push up and back with the feet and legs. The arms should swing beyond the head, clear of the water. The hands and arms should come together to form a streamlined shape. The back should arch and the whole body should be clear of the water.

Entry There should be a smooth entry led by the hands, then with straight arms, the head in line, followed by the hips and legs and pointed feet.

Transition to Swim There should be a streamlined glide under the surface with the hand and head directing the body towards the surface before the 15m marker. The feet should begin a dolphin then flutter kick and continue until the start of the first arm pull. One arm should pull for a smooth transition into full stroke at the surface, with the legs moving to an alternate action without any hesitation. The head should break the surface before the 15m marker. As for butterfly starts, swimmers should be encouraged to take full advantage of the '15m rule', according to age, skill and fitness.

Turn (Figs 47a–g)

Flags to Wall There should be no interruption of the stroke cycle during the last 5m. The flags should be used to check strokes and the head should not turn to look at the wall. There should be a continuous strong kick.

On the Wall There should be a positive rotation on to the front at the appropriate distance from the wall. There should be a smooth, fast forward flip to place the feet on the wall, before any momentum is lost.

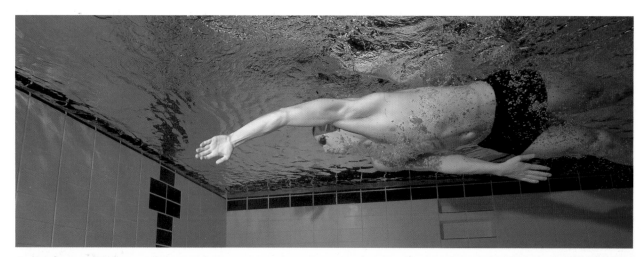

Fig 47a, b, c, d, e, f, g
Backstroke turn sequence.

Fig 48 Backstroke finish.

Push-Off There should be a strong push from the feet and legs as the hands are placed above the head ready for the stretch to a streamlined position. There should be a streamlined glide under the surface, with the hands and head directing the body smoothly towards the surface.

Transition to Swim The feet should kick just before the body starts to slow down. One arm should pull for a smooth transition into full stroke at the surface. The swimmer should not breathe during the first stroke cycle.

Finish (Fig 48)

There should be no interruption of the stroke cycle during the last 5m. The flags should be used, the head should not turn to look at the wall, and there should be a continuous strong kick. The finish should be positively registered with one hand, lying flat on the back at full stretch.

CHAPTER 10

BREASTSTROKE

Background

The breaststroke is often described as the most difficult swimming stroke to master. All leg and arm movements must be made simultaneously, and this is unlike everything else in the daily life of the human body. Except for the start, and the first stroke and kick after each turn, a part of the head must break the surface of the water during each stroke and kick cycle. The arm pull is performed in front of the body and is not as powerful as in the other strokes. The leg kick is a 'whip-like' action, usually very powerful, and is the main source of propulsion for the stroke.

The breaststroke has always been the most controversial stroke in swimming because of ongoing arguments over what constitutes legal or illegal technique. The Berlin Olympics in 1936 saw one of the first attempts at incorporating the then-controversial butterfly stroke into the Women's 200m Breaststroke event; a few swimmers were recovering their arms above the water rather than under, to save time and energy. Even having a separate stroke did not end the controversy. Six swimmers were disqualified in Breaststroke competition in the Melbourne Games because of different interpretations of what was a breaststroke and what was not. One Japanese swimmer found another loophole by swimming breaststroke underwater, finding that this was faster than swimming on the surface; after 1956, underwater swimming was banned from Breaststroke competition. The controversy continues to the present day, with competitors disqualified at the 2004 Athens Olympics for 'illegal' butterfly kicking at the starts and turns.

Successful exponents of modern breaststroke have a very streamlined body

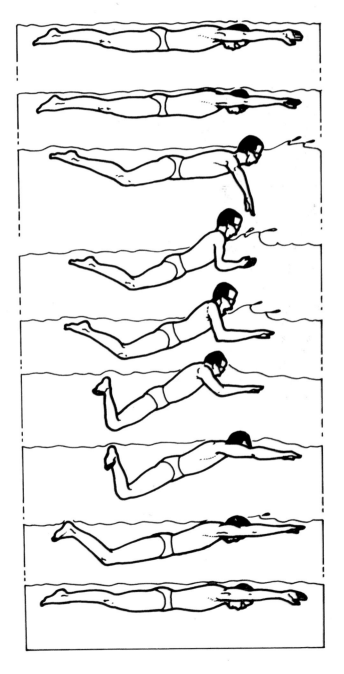

Fig 49a Breaststroke, side view.

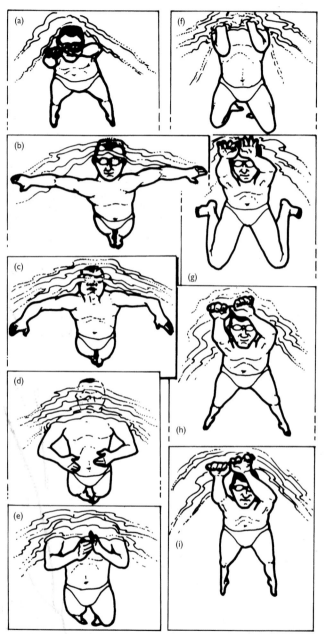

LEFT: *Fig 49b Breaststroke, front view.*

BELOW: *Fig 50 Breaststroke body position.*

position, maximizing the propulsive elements of the arms and legs. Notable examples of this are Liesl Jones and Kosuke Kitajima.

Technique

Body Position

The body should lie in a flat, horizontal, streamlined position; this will change during the stroke cycle as the breath is taken and just before stretching forward. There should be an undulating, wave-like flow during the stroke cycle. The body should achieve a stretched and streamlined position at the end of the kick (see Fig 50).

Feet and Legs

Recovery
The knees should bend, moving the lower legs towards the back of thigh (see Fig 51). The heels should go as close to the seat as possible, staying under the water surface, with the knees about hip-width apart (see Fig 52). The knees should not be brought up under the hips or stomach. Lowering the hips a little facilitates this.

Catch
Both feet should be pulled upwards and outwards into the critical 'dorsi-flexed' position. The feet must be outside the knees (see Fig 53). A very common mistake is to bring the feet up 'inside' the knees, thus significantly reducing the propulsion (see Fig 54). This is primarily a fault caused by inappropriate teaching practices in the early stages; instructions such as 'kick like a frog' should be avoided at all costs.

Propulsion
The feet should kick back, round and down in a fast 'whipping' action, with the soles and inside borders pressing on the water until they come together with the legs straight (see Figs 55a and 55b).

Fig 51 Breaststroke kick recovery.

Fig 52 Initiation of breaststroke kick.

Fig 53 Breaststroke kick catch.

Fig 54 Poor execution of breaststroke kick.

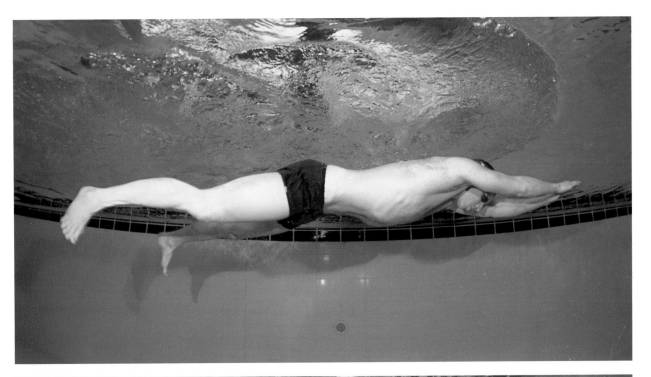

Fig 55a, b Finish of breaststroke kick.

Hands and Arms

Catch

The hands should face outwards and downwards and press sideways in a sculling-type action, to a point just wide of the shoulders (see Fig 49b).

Propulsion

The hands should lead the forearms in a vigorous downward and inward circling action, bringing the hands close together under the chest (see Fig 56). The hands should face each other, with the elbows and upper arms following in, to begin the recovery.

Recovery

There should be no hesitation between propulsion and recovery as the hands and forearms move smoothly and continuously under the chin towards the recovery stretch (see Figs 57a–c).

Breathing

The breath should be taken in as the mouth is lifted clear of the water as the shoulders and head rise. The exhalation can either be explosive or a steady trickle during the kick (see Fig 58).

Timing

There should be a moment when the complete body is in a stretched, streamlined position, with the head in line, at the conclusion of the kick (see Fig 59). The hands should start the catch before the legs begin to recover. The kick should start slightly before the hands start to stretch forwards. There should be a breath taken once in each stroke cycle.

Breaststroke Start, Turn and Finish

Start

Control The swimmer should be able to demonstrate complete control at the front of the block, with no movement or rolling. Fig 60 shows the 'take your marks' position for a track start on the blocks. Unlike the grab start (see Fig 36), the track start (as the name suggests) has one foot in front of the other. The front foot has the toes over the edge as before, with the weight further back towards the rear foot. A vigorous pull with the arms initiates the flight after the starting signal.

Fig 56 Breaststroke pull.

OPPOSITE PAGE: *Fig 57a, b, c Breaststroke pull and recovery.*

THIS PAGE:
LEFT: *Fig 58*
Breaststroke breathing.

BELOW: *Fig 59*
Breaststroke streamlining.

OPPOSITE PAGE:
Fig 60 Track start.

Reaction The swimmer should have a fast response to the signal.

Signal to Entry The swimmer should thrust up and out from the starting block. The swimmer should achieve optimum height and distance. A track start is characterized by fast reactions and a steeper flight/entry.

Entry There should be a smooth entry led by the hands then with straight arms, the head in line, followed by the hips and legs, with the feet making a limited splash.

Transition to Swim There should be a streamlined glide under the surface, with the hands and head directing the body to a horizontal position. There should be one complete long stroke under the water, starting just before the body starts to slow down. As the hands are returned, close to the body, to a position above the head, the feet are raised in preparation to kick to the surface. As the feet begin the first kick, the hands and head direct the body towards the surface. As the head breaks the surface, the hands begin the second arm cycle.

Turn

The breaststroke turn is almost identical to that on butterfly apart from the different stroke techniques on the way in and out of the wall. The 'on the wall' and 'push-off' sequence shown in Fig 44 is entirely the same for both strokes.

Flag to Wall The stroke length should not change during the last 5m. The body should be streamlined at the touch, with elbows slightly bent and there should be no extra glide. There should be a two-handed touch as per the laws.

On the Wall There should be a good tuck and pivot action, with the head staying low. One arm should move over the water and the other below the water as both feet are placed on the wall with the knees bent.

Push Off The arms should be placed above the head, under the surface of the water, as the feet and legs push. There should be a streamlined glide under the surface, with the hands and head directing the body to a horizontal position.

Transition to Swim There should be one complete long stroke under the water, starting just before the body starts to slow down. As the hands are returned, close to the body, to a position above the head, the feet should be raised in preparation for the kick to the surface. As the feet begin the first kick, the hands and head should direct the body towards the surface. As the head breaks the surface, the hands should begin the second arm cycle.

Finish

The stroke length should not change during the last 5m. The body should be streamlined at the touch, with elbows straight and no extra glide. The finish should be positively registered with a two-handed touch as per the laws.

CHAPTER II

FREESTYLE

Background

Characterized by its long overhead stroke and vigorous 'flutter' kick, the freestyle is the fastest and most powerful of the swimming strokes. The competitions of the 1800s were tame affairs, with swimmers limited to the breaststroke and sidestrokes to keep their heads above water. But the appearance of two North American Indians at a swim meet in London in the mid-nineteenth century, and the travels to South America of an Englishman some three decades later, revolutionized the sport for ever.

The American Indian swimmers shocked the British in 1844 with their dramatic arm motions, which were likened to windmills on the water. The flailing over-arm stroke that they brought to England was in fact centuries old, used for many generations by the inhabitants of the Americas, West Africa and some Pacific islands. The sidestroke, in which the swimmer would lie on one side, was soon modified to become an over-arm sidestroke. One arm was recovered above the water for increased arm speed and the legs were squeezed together in an uncoordinated action.

It was John Trudgeon who developed the hand-over-hand stroke, which was then given the name 'the Trudgeon stroke'. He copied the stroke from South American Indians and introduced it in England in 1873. Each arm recovered out of the water as the body rolled from side to side. The swimmer did a scissors kick with every two arm strokes. This stroke was the forerunner of the frontcrawl. Kick variations included different multiples of scissors kicks or alternating scissors and flutter kicks. The inefficiency of the early Trudgeon kick led Australian Richard Cavill to try new methods. He introduced a stroke that he had observed natives of the

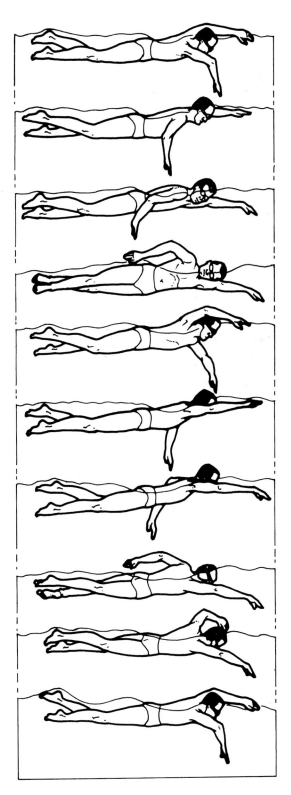

Fig 61 Freestyle, side view.

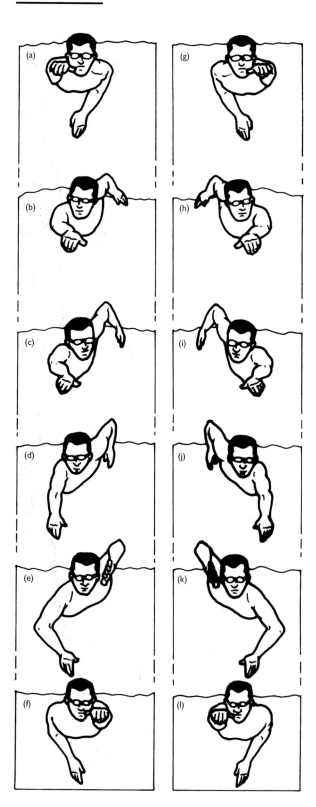

Fig 62 Freestyle, front view.

Solomon Islands using, which combined an up-and-down kick with an alternating overarm stroke. Cavill taught the new technique to his six sons, who all went on to be championship swimmers. This new style was first used in competition in 1902. When asked to describe the new style, one of Cavill's sons said it was 'like crawling through the water'. It became known as the 'Australian crawl', but the stroke is now better known as the frontcrawl or freestyle

Although swum with the head up for a time, the freestyle is the swimming stroke that has changed the least over the years. It also remains the fastest stroke, with swimmers racing at top speeds of over 2m per second.

Technique

Body Position

The body should be horizontal, straight and streamlined, with the hips slightly lower than the shoulders. The surface of the water should cut the head near the normal hairline. The eyes should look forwards and down at the pool floor, a short distance ahead (see Fig 63). There should be continuous rotation of the shoulders and upper body. The head should remain central and steady, except for a smooth turning to the side to breathe.

Leg Action

The feet and legs should maintain a steady, positive kicking action. At the bottom of the kick, the heel and sole of the foot should make a slight splash, just breaking the surface, with the knee slightly bent. The legs should move vertically, passing close to each other (see Fig 64). The action should originate at the hips, pass down through the legs, finishing with a strong positive movement of the feet and lower legs against the water.

Fig 63 Freestyle body position.

Fig 64 Freestyle kick.

Hands and Arms

Entry

The hands should slide into the water, with elbows slightly bent. The hand should enter between the shoulder and head, angled slightly outwards. The thumb and finger enter first, followed by the palm, wrist, forearm and elbow (see Fig 65).

Propulsion

The hand should exert force in the water, with the palm pressing out and down. The hand should then pitch slightly inwards, sweeping towards the centre of the body with the thumb edge leading. The elbow should point towards the side of the pool. At the midline of the body, the fingers should point towards the bottom of the pool and push back towards the legs (see Figs 66a and 66b). The thumb should pass very close to the leg. Classically, this is described as an 'S-shaped' pull, but underwater analysis of top swimmers shows that, at best, the 'S-shape' is very flat. In some cases, a very direct, backward pull is used, with the hand seemingly 'fixed' on the water. Conceptually, for young swimmers, it may be better to describe the action as 'backwards under the shoulder that is pulling, without crossing the midline'.

THIS PAGE:
Fig 65 Freestyle entry.

OPPOSITE PAGE:
Fig 66a, b Freestyle pull.

Recovery

The elbow should lead into the recovery phase, followed by the wrists and hand. The forearm should move close to the head and the hand should be below the elbow towards the entry point (see Fig 67).

Breathing

There should be a smooth and controlled turn of the head to the side with the side of the face in the water. The breath should be inhaled from a small trough created by the head, just below the true water level. The breath should be exhaled into the water. Breathing should be an established regular pattern in the stroke cycle.

Timing

Timing will vary slightly from swimmer to swimmer but should always be consistent and continuous with control.

Freestyle Start, Turn and Finish

Start

Control The swimmer should be able to demonstrate complete control at the front of the block, with no movement or rolling.

Reaction The swimmer should have a fast response to the signal.

Signal to Entry The swimmer should thrust up and out from the starting block. The swimmer should achieve optimum height and distance.

Entry There should be a smooth entry led by the hands, then with straight arms and the head in line, followed by the hips and legs, with the feet making little splash.

Transition to Swim There should be a streamlined glide under the surface, with the hands and head directing the body smoothly towards the surface. The feet should kick just before the body starts to slow down. One arm should pull for a smooth transition into full stroke at the surface. The swimmer should not breathe during the first stroke cycle.

Turn

Flags to Wall There should be no interruption of the stroke cycle during the last 5m. There should be a continuous strong kick. The hand and head should lead down into the turning movement.

Fig 67 Freestyle recovery.

On the Wall There should be a smooth fast flip, placing the feet on the wall with knees bent.

Push Off The legs should provide a strong powerful push as the hands, arms and body stretch to a streamlined position. There should be a streamlined glide under the surface, with the hands and head directing the body smoothly towards the surface.

Transition to Swim The feet should kick just before the body starts to slow down. One arm should pull for a smooth transition into full stroke at the surface. The swimmer should not breathe during the first stroke cycle.

Finish

There should be no interruption of the stroke cycle during the last 5m. The swimmer should not breathe during the last 5m and there should be a continuous strong kick. The finish should be positively registered with the hand stretched out in front and the head still down.

CHAPTER 12

INDIVIDUAL MEDLEY

According to most leading coaches, the Individual Medley (usually shortened to 'IM') is the 'fifth stroke' of swimming and should be considered as much in its own right as a combination of the four recognized strokes. Performed in the standard order of Butterfly-Backstroke-Breaststroke-Freestyle, the 'IM' is the most rigorous of swimming tests. As a foundation for progressing to excellence in any of the four main strokes, the medley should be used as the cornerstone of training programmes in age-group swimmers. It offers extensive possibilities for swimmers and coaches in terms of conditioning, variation, challenge and achievement.

As the focus of this section of the book is on technique, the illustrations that follow are concerned with the transitions from one stroke to another in the IM. All other technical information for the four strokes applies equally to the medley as to the individual stroke in question.

Transitions

Fly–Back IM Turn

This is the easiest of the three IM transitions. As the swimmer comes in on his front and goes out on his back, there is little to do other than bring the knees up and effect a powerful push-off. The contact time between the hands touching and feet leaving should be as short as possible. Using the 15m rule on the backstroke should again be encouraged.

Back–Breast IM Turn

There are a couple of possibilities to switch strokes in the middle of an IM race. Some

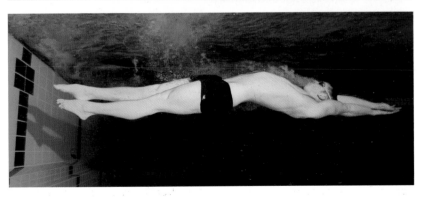

Fig 68 Fly–Back IM turn from the side, underwater.

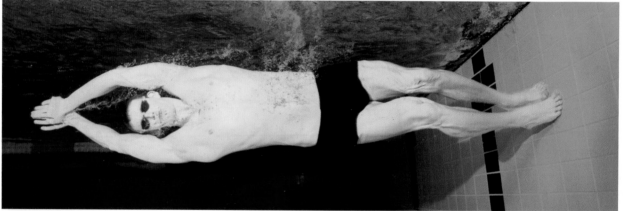
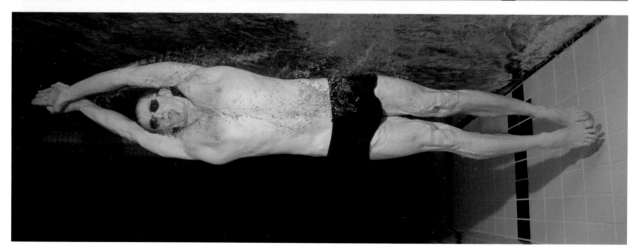

Fig 69a Back–Breast IM turn from the side, underwater.

swimmers will use the simple 'swivel turn' (see Fig 69a). This is useful because a breath can be taken as the mouth clears the water during the 'on-the-wall' phase. A potentially faster turn is shown in Fig 69b, with a 'back flip' performed as the hand touches. This may change direction more quickly, but the loss of a sustained breath may be crucial to the physiological demands of the race in its later stages. For this reason, most swimmers use the swivel turn on the 400IM and the flip turn on a 200IM race. Coaches and swimmers should practise both throughout the season.

Breast–Free IM turn

The standard turn described for butterfly and breaststroke (see Fig 37) is the turn used for the last stroke transition in IM.

An important final point to make is that swimmers should 'settle' into the new stroke as quickly as possible after each change. This means that technique and stroke tempo should be established a few strokes into the new race segment. Swimmers who coast into and out of the transitions will lose valuable time and will fail to maximize their performance potential.

MEDLEY TOP TIPS

- To excel at the medley, the swimmer needs to be expert in all four strokes.
- Start with the 100IM for novice swimmers (aged 6–8); progress to the 200IM for pre-competitive levels (aged 9–12); progress to the 400IM as the base for competitive swimmers (aged 12 and older).
- Relate performance in all four strokes to IM performance, in other words, 50sec for the 100IM, 100sec for the 200IM and 200sec for the 400IM.
- Swimmers should do lots of 'switching' sets to practise linking the strokes and improve the transition turns.

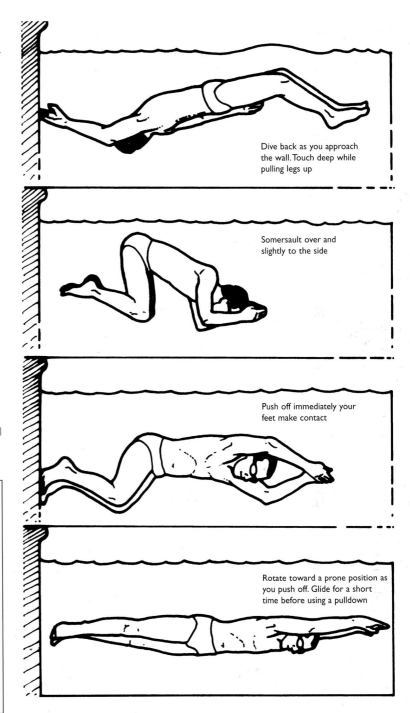

Dive back as you approach the wall. Touch deep while pulling legs up

Somersault over and slightly to the side

Push off immediately your feet make contact

Rotate toward a prone position as you push off. Glide for a short time before using a pulldown

Fig 69b Back–Breast IM turn.

PART 3

TRAINING

CHAPTER 13

METHODS AND PRINCIPLES OF TRAINING

Training Methods

There are four general methods of pool training available to the coach and swimmer: Swim (full stroke practice), Kick (legs only), Pull (arms only) and Drill. However, with this in addition to the four strokes and individual medley, the possibility of both short- and long-course swimming, plus the myriad of equipment options on the market, all adds up to a challenging and complex recipe of training, stroke development and race preparation.

For guidance on the four strokes and IM, and for the outline on the use of drills for a variety of aims, see the previous chapters. The following section focuses on the use of Kicking and Pulling as training methods.

There is no easy formula to the prescription of swimming training and it is as much art as science, but there are some general principles that can assist in maximizing the preparation opportunities available.

Kicking

Whether it is taking full advantage of the 15m underwater off starts and turns, or generating power from the legs on the last 50m of a race, the importance of kicking on swimming performance should not be under-estimated. For example, a short-course 100m Backstroke race could be swum with up to 60m (4 x 15m per length) underwater. Perfecting this opportunity does not happen by accident, nor does it occur overnight. It is developed over time by careful planning and progressions, and no small amount of commitment by those involved. Kicking is the slowest method of training, but this

should not negate its impact upon performance. A swimmer who improves his kicking ability is almost always a swimmer who swims faster.

Kicking may not contribute greatly to 'direct' propulsion in all but the breaststroke, but enhanced body positions and reduced drag as a result of effective kicking can significantly contribute to 'indirect propulsion' in the other three strokes.

KEY POINT

A variety of options are available to coaches in designing kick sets and practices:

- With or without a kickboard?
- What size/shape of kickboard?
- With or without fins?
- What size/shape of fins?
- Kick on the front/side or back?
- What distance, rest and speed to use?

Pulling

As with kicking, the aims and types of pulling are varied. Some aspects of pulling are easier to perform than others due to the technique and flow of the strokes, for example, freestyle as opposed to butterfly with a pull buoy. Since the primary aim of pulling is to isolate and condition the arms, practices and training should be centred on this purpose.

On butterfly, care should be taken to ensure that stroke mechanics are not compromised by pulling large distances with a pull buoy. All backstroke pulling should be done with a band only – no pull buoy should be used. Paddle shapes and

OPPOSITE PAGE:
Fig 70 Kicking practices on all four strokes.

sizes are at the discretion of the coach/swimmer. Breaststroke pull with a buoy should be done sparingly, as with butterfly, and never to the detriment of overall stroke mechanics. (Fly kick and breaststroke pull are a popular alternative.) Freestyle pull probably offers the greatest variety in terms of training options, but coaches and swimmers should be wary of over-using this method of training instead of improving full stroke swim.

KEY POINT

A variety of options are available to coaches in designing pull sets and practices:

- With or without paddles?
- What size/shape of paddles?
- With or without pull buoy?
- What size/shape of pull buoy?
- With or without a band?
- What distance, rest and speed to use?

Training Emphasis

There are many different labels given to swimming training, some of which differ in substance, while others are simply name changes. In general, the three main areas of training emphasis coincide with the three energy systems: aerobic; anaerobic and alactic. Coaches, scientists and authors around the world have come up with countless labels for 'training zones', 'training systems', 'training categories' and so on, but

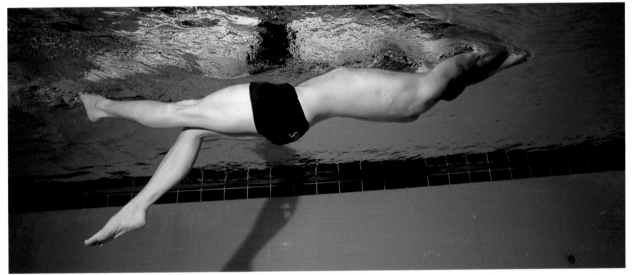

Fig 71 Training intensity sheet.

NAME	EXPLANATION	SET LENGTH	REST INTERVALS	WEEKLY VOLUME	HEARTRATE GUIDE
Warm-up and Swim-down	Preparation for session (physical and mental) Recovery	600–1,500m (15–25min)	5–30sec max.	min of 15%	**Prog to 50 beats below max**
Basic Aerobic	Slowest speed in training, technique work, long distance swims and drills	2,000–8,000m (25–120min)	10–30sec, not full recovery	up to 45%	**50–30 beats below max**
Threshold	Improvements in aerobic capacity, without overstressing system	1,500–3,000m (25–40min)	10–40sec	up to 25%	**30–20 beats below max**
Overload	Just above threshold to stress improvements in VO_2max	1,000–1,600m (15–25min)	1:1 work:rest ratio	up to 15%	**20 below– max HR**
Lactate Tolerance	Improving buffering capacity and pain of acidosis (passive rest)	300–800m (20–40min)	1–5min passive recovery	up to 7%	**Not relevant**
Lactate Production	Improving ability to finish races as fast as possible (active rest)	200–600m (20–40min)	1–5min active recovery	up to 7%	**Not relevant**
Pure Speed	Fastest possible speeds in training (with and without aids)	200–600m (20–40min)	Full recovery between reps	up to 7%	**Not relevant**

they have all come back to these three fundamental areas.

Within each energy system, there are different sub-types of training and these generally give their names to the types of training that are common across most swimming programmes: aerobic sets, threshold sets, overload sets, lactate sets and so on. It is suggested that the simpler the system used, the better. Complicated zones and codified categories will do little to promote understanding by swimmers or coaches, and ultimately mean an overly complex system of planning, recording and monitoring.

See Fig 71 for a simple model of training emphasis. Details of training parameters such as volume, intensity and rest are given in sample sets.

Other forms of swimming, such as warming up and swimming down, are used in training, but these are not covered in detail here as there is little or no training effect to be gained from them. This is not to devalue their importance in any training programme. The following sections relate instead to the main focus areas.

Base Aerobic Training

Variously known as Zone 1, A1 or En-1, base aerobic training is the least intense training that swimmers do. It is also the type of training that covers the highest volume of work. Used mainly as maintenance and recovery training, base aerobic work is simply low-intensity endurance training, designed to improve sub-maximal cardiovascular efficiency and the use of oxygen in supplying energy to the working muscles.

A season-long feature of training programmes, the traditional pattern of conditioning work sees a 'base' of aerobic fitness being built from the beginning and developed with higher-intensity work as the season progresses.

---

3 X EFFECTS OF BASE AEROBIC TRAINING

1 Increased cardiac output.
2 Increased blood volume.
3 Improved blood shunting.

SAMPLE BASIC AEROBIC TRAINING SET

(Early season for a 14-year-old girl 400-IM swimmer)

100 Fly
200 as 100 Fly–Back
100 Back
200 as 100 Back–Breast
100 Breast
200 as 100 Breast–Free
100 Free
Repeat x 3 with 20sec rests throughout
(3,000m)

GUIDELINES FOR BASIC AEROBIC SETS

• Minimum: 20min.
• Maximum: as the session allows.
• Short rests (5–30sec), according to repeat distance.
• Repeat distances of 50m and upwards.
• Low- to medium-intensity efforts.

Base aerobic training can be done on all four strokes, although some swimmers may find it difficult to swim butterfly 'aerobically' at this low intensity.

Threshold Training

The term 'anaerobic threshold' is often derided by physiologists, who say that it wrongly implies the end of something (aerobic work) and the start of something else (anaerobic work). The acronym OBLA (onset of blood lactate accumulation) is suggested as a more accurate alternative. Although some swimming coaches do use this term, 'anaerobic threshold' is very much a fixture in the vocabulary of coaches. It is more important to do the training correctly than to argue about the semantics.

In simple terms, this type of training is more intense than base aerobic work, but its physiological effects are very similar in generating cardio-respiratory and muscle-cell adaptations. Threshold training is used throughout the season and on all four strokes. It is also used as a reference point for prescribing other intensities of training, for example, 'swim 2 seconds per 100 slower than threshold speed'. The blend of volume and intensity of threshold training is an important marker for the coach: too little and the adaptations will stagnate, too much and the swimmer may struggle to cope with excessive amounts.

Overload Training

This is the highest-intensity aerobic work possible and, as the name implies, is very taxing. One of its other names is 'VO$_2$max training', because it stresses maximal aerobic work. Overload sets should not be repeated too many times in a week and it takes good recovery strategies to be ready to 'go again'. Training benefits from overload work are mainly aerobic, but modest anaerobic advantages can also be gained. Swimmers should perform this work on their main stroke(s) to gain

---

3 X EFFECTS OF THRESHOLD TRAINING

1 Increased use of aerobic capacity.
2 Increased removal of lactate.
3 Increased levels of mitochondria and myoglobin.

SAMPLE THRESHOLD TRAINING SET

(Short-course, pre-competition phase for 16-year-old male 200 Back swimmer)

4 x (8 x 100 Back), extra 30sec between sets
Set 1, prog 1–4 to threshold pace; hold 5–8 at threshold on 1.40
Set 2, hold 1–8 at threshold on 1.40
Set 3, hold 1–8 at threshold on 1.40
Set 4 hold 1–4 at threshold on 1.40; prog 5–8 to best effort on 2.00
(3,200m)

NB: progressing to threshold in Set 1 establishes the correct pace.
The extra 30sec between sets is more psychological than physiological.
The extra progression at the end is a good indicator of working at the correct pace, i.e. swimmers SHOULD be able to swim faster.

GUIDELINES FOR THRESHOLD SETS

- Minimum: 20min.
- Maximum: 60min (for elite distance swimmers).
- Short rests (10–30sec), according to repeat distance.
- Repeat distances of 50–400m.
- Medium-intensity efforts.

---

3 X EFFECTS OF OVERLOAD TRAINING

1 Increased VO$_2$max.
2 Increased buffering capacity.
3 Increased number of capillaries.

SAMPLE OVERLOAD TRAINING SET

(Long-course, competition phase for senior female 400 Freestyle swimmer)

3 x (5 x 200) F/c on 3.00
Set 1, progress 1–5 to 'best pace'
Set 2 hold 'best average'
Set 3 hold 'best average' (3,000m)

GUIDELINES FOR OVERLOAD SETS

- 20–45min long.
- 1:1 work:rest ratio for short repeats (close to this for longer reps).
- Repeat distances of 50–300m.
- High-intensity efforts.

---

maximum benefits from the specificity of training principle.

From the example of the backstroke swimmer above, the threshold training set of 4 x (8 x 100) ends with an overload effort, as the last 4 x 100 were progressively faster than threshold pace.

Lactate-Tolerance Training

Lactate-tolerance training involves swimming at high-intensity efforts over short repeat distances with a passive (and incomplete) recovery. By creating a build-up of lactic acid (lactate), one key training effect is improved buffering capacity of the muscles. Lactate-tolerance training is a very stressful form of training, both physically and mentally, and is usually introduced into the training programme once a good level of conditioning has been reached. Recovery from this training takes around 48 hours, so two to three times a week are the maximum amounts possible. For maximum performance benefits, swimmers should do this type of training on their No.1 stroke(s).

Allied to lactate-tolerance training is 'lactate-removal' training. As there is no active recovery during tolerance sets (the rest intervals will not allow this), the build-up of lactate needs to be removed immediately afterwards – hence the name. Essentially, it is recovery work, but, in the context of repeated training and competition swims, the ability to remove lactic acid effectively from the muscles becomes a very important part of the swimmers' arsenal against fatigue and under-performance.

The example below shows a lactate-tolerance set and a lactate-removal set.

---

3 X EFFECTS OF LACTATE-TOLERANCE TRAINING

1 Improved tolerance of acidosis.
2 Improved removal of lactate.
3 Improved rate of anaerobic metabolism.

SAMPLE LACTATE TOLERANCE TRAINING SET

(Competition phase for senior male 200 Butterfly swimmer)

4 x 25 Fly on 40 prog effort, check speed and stroke count
4 x 50 Fly on 1.00 prog effort 1–4
12 x 75 Fly on 3.30 max effort
(1,100m)
Twice through the following:
4 x 50 on 50 as Free/25 Form
2 x 100 on 1.45 as 50 Free/50 Form
1 x 200 Free on 3.15
2 x 100 on 1.45 as 50 Form/50 Free
4 x 50 on 50 as 25 Form/25 Free
Checking recovery levels and concentrating on technique, not effort
(2,000m)

GUIDELINES FOR TOLERANCE SETS

- Approx 300–800m of 'tolerance work'.
- Work:rest ratio of 1:3 or 4 with passive recovery.
- Repeat distances of 25–150m.
- Maximum-intensity efforts.
- 'Removal' sets should be upwards of 1,600m long.

Lactate-Production Training

Sometimes known as 'lactate power' or 'anaerobic capacity' training, the key difference between this and tolerance training is the presence of active recovery between maximal-effort swims. Research has shown that doing this type of 'sprint' training can improve capacity by up to 20 per cent in just eight weeks. Its aims (and effects) are similar to those of tolerance work in terms of improved buffering and energy release, but the active recovery elements mean that the physical and mental stress on the swimmer is slightly reduced.

It is possible for this type of training to be done every day, as recovery time is less of an issue, but in practice coaches will usually prescribe it two to four times a week, to balance out the other work being done. For maximum performance

---

3 X EFFECTS OF LACTATE-PRODUCTION TRAINING

- Increased rate of anaerobic metabolism.
- Increased sprinting speed.
- Increased muscular power.

SAMPLE LACTATE-PRODUCTION TRAINING SET

(Short-course, mid-season for 16-year-old female 100 Breaststroke swimmer)

25 max/25 recovery on 1.30
50 max/50 recovery on 3.00
75 max/125 recovery on 6.00
Repeat x 4
(1,400m)

All max efforts done from a dive start

GUIDELINES FOR PRODUCTION SETS

- Approx 300–800m of 'production work'.
- Work:rest ratio of 1:4 or 5 with active recovery.
- Repeat distances of 25–100m.
- Maximum-intensity efforts.

---

benefits, swimmers should also do this type of training on their No.1 stroke(s).

Authors' note: There is some confusion in the literature about what constitutes lactate-tolerance, lactate-removal and lactate-production training and this is replicated in the varied programmes of many coaches and swimmers. Apart from a desire to see everyone 'speaking the same language', there is nothing wrong in this if the way the work is programmed has the desired effects. An understanding of the physiological concepts and mechanisms is more important than slavishly following conventions that are not fundamentally understood.

Pure Speed Training

Also known as 'power' or 'sprint' training, this is the fastest type of work done by swimmers. It can be even faster than race speeds with the assistance of paddles, fins or other devices such as tubing or towing machines. The scheduling of pure speed training is discussed in Chapter 14, but it is best done when swimmers are fresh and not suffering from the fatiguing effects of other forms of training. It can be done on all forms of training (Swim, Kick, Pull or Drills) and is thought to offer swimmers the best chance to transfer any strength

---

3 X EFFECTS OF PURE SPEED TRAINING

1 Increased stroke power.
2 Increased rate and pattern of fibre recruitment.
3 Increased rate of force production.

SAMPLE PURE SPEED TRAINING SET

(Taper phase for 15-year-old female sprinter)
4 x 15m on 45
1 x 100 as 25 drill/swim
4 x 20m on 60
1 x 150 as 50 swim/drill
4 x 25m on 1.15
1 x 200 as 50 drill/swim
Repeat x 2
(480m speed work)

and power gains on dry land into the pool environment.

Pure speed training can be done throughout the season, every day if desired, and, if done properly, does not deplete vital glycogen stores required for other training sets. Swimmers should focus pure speed training on their main stroke(s) and, although it can be done faster than race speed, care should be taken to practise race stroke rates and patterns at all times.

GUIDELINES FOR PURE SPEED SETS

- Approx 200–600m of 'speed' work.
- Work:rest ratio of 1:6 with active or passive recovery.
- Repeat distances of 10–25m.
- Maximum intensity efforts.
- Practise race stroke rates.

Training Sets

Most swimming training is done on an 'interval' basis. First conceived in Germany in the 1930s, interval training has become the predominant form of training in most sports and is governed by the acronym 'DIRT'. This has been modified over the years and different coaches have used the acronym to suit their needs, but it generally stands for the following:

- D – the distance swum;
- I – the intensity of the work;
- R – the number of repetitions to be performed; and
- T – the time (or interval) taken for each swim.

Other acronyms have been used (including ANDFIR, as in Aim, Number, Distance, Frequency, Intensity, Rest), but the enduring appeal of DIRT lies in its simplicity and applicability. Within the 'interval training' framework, there are a number of other training set types.

Slow or Fast Interval Sets

Governed by the amount of rest in the set and the pace of the swims, these are the simplest and most common training sets. A 'fast interval' set would be 20 × 100m on a 2.00 rest plus swim time. A 'slow interval' set would be over a longer distance, for example, 6 × 400m on a 5.00 turnaround.

Fartlek Swims

Fartlek literally means 'speedplay' in German, and fartlek swims are derived from langlauf training in cross-country skiing. They are generally longer in duration and involve swims at varying speeds according to the stage of the season and design of the set. For example, the swimmer might be required to swim 4 × 800m with every sixth 25 fast on the first 800, every fifth 25 fast on the second 800, every fourth 25 fast on the third 800, and every third 25 fast on the fourth 800. Coaches will often vary the strokes to be swum fast, for example, in the above case, swimming the 800s on freestyle with the fast 25s on fly.

Over-Distance Swims

Usually part of early-season conditioning, over-distance swims are (as the name implies) longer than race distance and used at a fairly low intensity. The aim is to facilitate basic aerobic conditioning and recovery from higher-intensity work. In the 4 × 800m example above, this could also be an 'over-distance' set for 100/200m swimmers (with or without the fartlek sections).

Pyramid Sets

Sometimes also known as Hungarian sets, these are usually symmetrical in design and may involve manipulation of some or all of the DIRT variables. For example, 6 × 50 on 40, 6 × 100 on 80, 6 × 200 on 2.40, 6 × 100 on 90, 6 × 50 on 45. On the 'way

up' to 200, the turnaround time is an average of 40sec per 50, and on the 'way back down' to the 50s it is an average of 45sec per 50. Coaches would expect swimmers to hold a faster average time for the increased rest given.

Progressive Sets

Again commonly used to vary the pace of swims, progressive sets are very popular in training and testing situations alike. For example, a set of 4 × (8 × 100 f/c), with each set even paced, but faster than the previous one, could be used for conditioning and to monitor progress throughout the season; as the swimmers get fitter, the average times in each section of the set improve. Another way of designing a progressive set is to swim each repeat faster than the previous one and repeat this cycle a number of times, for example, 5 × (4 × 200 progress 1–4). The challenge is to be able to maintain the pattern not just once but five times. A further advantage of this type of training is that it covers a range of training intensities and, therefore, a number of physiological stimuli.

Broken Swims

Almost exclusively the preserve of race-preparation training, the concept of 'broken swims' is to provide an opportunity to practice race-pace swimming without performing the full race distance every time. For example, a common 'broken swim' for 200m events is to do 4 × 50m with 10sec rest between 50s.

STAR TIP

There are several variations of the training themes, and adding in the equipment described in Chapter 2 (paddles, fins, kickboards, pullbuoys, and so on) leads to many possibilities for the innovative coach to design a varied and challenging training programme.

Principles of Training

Ultimately, the correct application of all training methods is governed by the use of the appropriate 'Principles of Training':

1 Individuality.
2 Adaptation.
3 Overload.
4 Progression.
5 Specificity.
6 Variation.
7 Reversibility.
8 Balance.
9 Long-term planning.

Individuality

Every individual is different and will respond to training in a unique way. This may seem obvious, but research conducted in the UK, by coach Ian Wright, has shown that most swimming programmes are conducted on a group or squad basis and that only the very highest-level performers have anything close to an individualized programme. There are many reasons for this, but it is primarily to do with resources. Nevertheless, acknowledging the individual response to training is a fundamental tenet of designing and implementing an effective training programme.

Adaptation

Training has an effect on the human body, indeed, the very purpose of training is to have the desired effect on the body or,

more specifically, on its processes. The effects are governed by the principle of adaptation. Placing the systems in the body under stress will produce responses associated with the type of training performed. For example, an adaptation to aerobic training is a reduced sub-maximal heart rate for a given workload. Some

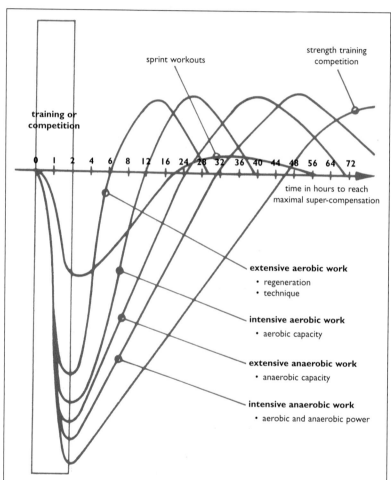

Training types	Extensive Endurance	Intensive Endurance	Sprints/ Short Sets	Extensive Anaerobic Training	Extensive Strength Training	Intensive Anaerobic Training	Intensive Strength Training/ Competition
From	8	24	30	36	40	40	48
To	12	30	40	48	60	60	72

Fig 72 Super-compensation model.

> ### STAR TIP
>
> For effective training adaptations, the following must be in place:
>
> • correct training;
> • nutrients for growth and repair of tissues; and
> • sufficient rest for the growth and repair to take place.

adaptations take place in a matter of days, while others may take weeks or months.

Overload

Probably the most important principle of all, the concept of overload in training is also one of the oldest of the principles. In order for adaptations to take place, the stress on the body's systems must be sufficiently significant for physiological changes to occur, in other words, it must be greater than 'usual'. The same stimuli will not provoke continued improvements and therefore the principle of overloading must be applied. There is a danger in overloading and it is the careful application of this principle that brings us to the next consideration – progression.

Progression

Often coupled with overload as a 'double-whammy' principle, the use of a progressive or 'step-wise' approach to training prescription is the most obvious application of periodization in action. Too much loading at once may result in over-training or injury, while too little may result in no improvements being made. Swimming is a sport in which it is easy to see the principles of progressive overload being used, for example, longer distances, less rest, more repetitions, faster effort and so on. The systematic treatment of training programmes in a structured and progressive manner is the result of careful and considered planning by effective coaches.

Specificity

Although another obvious principle, the use of specificity by swimming coaches is at times questionable. It is easy to note that regular running or cycling will not improve butterfly swimming performance, but research again shows that coaches are less than precise about their specific, individualized prescription of training. There is a mistaken belief among some

coaches that freestyle is the 'training stroke' and that somehow the benefits of training will transfer across to the other strokes. This is wrong! There is no evidence to support it. Coaches should consider the following four aspects when applying the principle of specificity:

1 The event.
2 The stroke.
3 The target speed.
4 The energy system demands of these combined.

Variation

As far as skill learning is concerned, the greater the range of opportunities given to swimmers, the greater the likelihood that they will improve. In training for physical capacity, the use of the variation principle can sometimes be overdone and care should be taken to use variety as a motivational tool rather than simply as an end in its own right.

Reversibility

Often simplified to 'if you don't use it, you lose it', this principle is more obvious after a period away from training. Swimmers soon discover how hard it is to gain fitness over a period of time, but how easy it is to lose it much more quickly.

Balance

Associated with the principle of variation, this principle recognizes that a swimmer cannot do everything at once. Successfully applying training principles requires as much art as science and the principle of balance is where the coach can be creative in the design and implementation of training.

Long-Term Planning

'It takes ten years of extensive practice to excel in anything', according to Nobel

Laureate H.A. Simon. This is never more true than in the field of training for sports performance. Translating the quote into the language of swimming training, this is three to four hours per day of deliberate practice for ten years and is supported by empirical and anecdotal evidence from successful swimmers.

For details of the Long-Term Athlete Development programme for swimming in Britain, see pages 25–9.

Training Effects

The physiological study of swimming training merits an entire book on its own. The aim of this short section is to summarize the contributions of physiological processes to swimming, outline the main training effects of the training types and methods, and discuss the factors that limit performance in swimming events.

Energy Systems and Performance

It is common to refer to sprints as 'anaerobic' and distance events as 'aerobic', but this is not entirely accurate from a physiological standpoint. Fig 73 illustrates the relative contributions of the three energy systems to swimming events and training sets. In keeping with advances in the study of exercise, aerobic processes are sub-divided into glucose and fat metabolism, in order to differentiate between the contributions each makes to energy supply. The percentages in Fig 73 are the author's interpretation of the available research and are based on the likely responses of senior 200–400m swimmers. Sprinters (better anaerobically) or more distance-oriented swimmers (better aerobically) will respond differently to the demands of swimming events. It should also be noted that the relative contributions of energy systems will also be affected by the strokes swum, the chronological age and the training age/status of the swimmer.

COMPETITION TIMES	RACE DISTANCES	% ATP-CP	% ANAEROBIC METABOLISM	Aerobic metabolism	
				% GLUCOSE METABOLISM	% FAT METABOLISM
10–15sec	25yd/m	50	50	Neg	Neg
19–30sec	50yd/m	20	60	20	Neg
40–60sec	100yd/m	10	55	35	Neg
1.30–2min	200yd/m	7	40	53	Neg
2–3min	200yd/m	5	40	55	Neg
4–6min	500yd (400m)	Neg	35	65	Neg
7–10min	900yd (800m)	Neg	25	73	2
10–12min	1,000yd (900m)	Neg	20	75	5
14–22min	1,650yd (1,500m)	Neg	15	78	7

Fig 73 Relative contributions of each phase of energy metabolism to various swimming races and practice repeats.

Limiting Factors in Performance

Summarized in Fig 74, the factors that significantly limit performance in training and competition vary according to the distance of the event and, consequently, the time it lasts, combined with the speed of the effort. The short, sprint events in swimming (50m on all strokes) are limited primarily by technique and the availability of energy sources for fast, powerful muscle contractions (ATP-CP). For 100–200m events, the limiting factors also include technique, but are much more concerned with delaying acidosis of the muscles and, once again, energy supply (anaerobic). For the longer events, of 400m and above, technique is still an important factor, as is acidosis again, and although energy supply is once more a factor, it is (by nature of the duration of the events) a combination of aerobic and anaerobic energy that produces the resultant performance. Daily training is limited mainly by the body's ability to replenish glycogen stores (see Chapter 16 on Nutrition) and the avoidance of injury.

25 and 50 races
1 Stroke technique.
2 Rate of anaerobic metabolism.
3 Amount of CP stored in working muscle fibres.

100 and 200 races
1 Stroke technique.
2 Ability to delay acidosis.
3 Rate of anaerobic metabolism.
4 Possibly the amount of CP stored in working muscle fibres.

Middle Distance and Distance Races
1 Stroke technique.
2 Ability to delay acidosis.
3 Rate of anaerobic metabolism.

Day-to-Day Training
1 Muscle glycogen depletion.
2 Muscle tissue injury.

Fig 74 Factors that limit performance in sprint, middle distance and distance swimming events.

CHAPTER 14

THE SESSION

It is generally conceded that the most important aspect of swimming emphasis should be skill. Small changes in stroking skill will translate into large changes in performance whereas moderate changes in fitness and psychology produce only small to modest improvements. Thus, the development of swimming skills should be the primary focus of training at all levels. However, that is not the most popular orientation, as the sport at large still embraces a priority for fitness development. Practice-session plans need to consider where technical and tactical skill training should occur to supplement fitness training so that the best learning will be produced. There is sufficient scientific information available to suggest that there is a particular order in which psychological and physiological experiences should occur in a session.

KEY POINT

The use of the term 'practice session' is a more accurate one than the more common 'training session'. The implication is that objectives other than just improving fitness are being sought.

The skill-learning capacity of an individual is moderated by his state of fitness. For the most efficient learning to occur, the fitness elements that are required for the performance of a skill need to exist in a sufficiently trained state to allow the skill to be performed adequately. For example, it would be difficult for a swimmer to attempt an 'elbows-up' position in freestyle, if he did not have sufficient body strength to be able to maintain a stable upper body position that only permitted rotation about the

longitudinal axis. The correct execution of the finer technique point is dependent upon having the postural strength to establish a solid foundation for its peripheral movements. If fatigue were to occur, it would interact with the skill precision and either cause performance deterioration or establish a need for a change in technique, neither of which are desirable on a regular basis. Thus, the most efficient development of technique will occur only when appropriate levels of fitness to support the technique have been attained.

The factors moderating the swimmer's rate of skill learning will determine what is included in a training session, how learning opportunities are distributed in a week's training, and what the learning objectives of the training phase are.

Factors Moderating Skill Learning

Age of the Learner

Skill-learning capacity varies with chronological and maturational age. One affects learning in a different way to the other. Infants, teenagers and the aged all have different potential capacities for learning. Two people with the same chronological age, but different maturational ages, learn at different rates. The amount of practice time allocated to learning will depend upon the interaction of both ages.

Training Stage

Strength, endurance and precision skills are all affected by training. The more training that has occurred, the better skill

learning is likely to be, given certain restrictions. In a group of swimmers, with different amounts of exposure to training in the same season, each individual should train on a programme that is appropriate for his stage. A single programme for a group assumes that all individuals are equal, but that assumption is not appropriate for efficient and productive coaching because it violates the important training principle of individuality. The state of fitness development will influence the level of skill precision that can be attained.

Training History

The longer the history of participation in sports, the greater is likely to be the number of skill elements that could be transferred to the early stages of learning a new skill. The richness of the history determines the level and initial speed of learning when new skills are attempted. The directions and activities used in coaching should be geared to each person's sporting background so that initial skill-learning experiences will be efficient.

Skill Level

A person's skill governs the potential rate of improvement. For example, it is much easier to improve from 50 to 40sec in a 50m backstroke than it is to improve from 40 to 30sec, although the absolute time changes are the same. Improvements of a specified magnitude will be more difficult to attain for more advanced athletes: the skill level of the athlete will determine the expectations for activity development. More training time for skill improvement will need to be provided for highly skilled swimmers to achieve noticeable performance changes.

Nature of the Skill

The more difficult or complex the skill, the greater will be the time required to reach specific proficiency levels. For programming training sessions, complicated skills and tactics should be allocated more time than simple activities. The concept of variable programming – assigning learning time opportunities that fit the requirements of the skill-learning experiences – needs to be introduced into the content of planning training.

KEY POINT

Strong reinforcement derived from learning experiences produces faster rates of skill acquisition than weak reinforcement. The reinforcers and incentives that exist in the training environment should be personalized and maximized.

KEY POINT

When an individual likes an activity, faster skill learning results than when an activity is not liked. A coach will have to be skilled in establishing the need and desirability for skill change/development.

Stimulus Variation

The more constant the learning environment, the faster the rate of skill acquisition. Training environments should provide consistent coaching situations, particularly for early stages of learning. Distraction reduces the rate of learning, particularly in the early stages of skill acquisition. Distractions should be eliminated through self-preoccupied instructional techniques. The cues for instruction and directions need to be as clear as possible.

Fatigue and Learning

The factors listed above indicate a need to avoid group instruction sessions when coaching skills. Group instruction methods have been perpetuated and may be easier to administer than individual instructional procedures, but this does not mean that they provide the best situation for learning to occur. Individualized training programmes may seem more difficult, but they have to be followed to produce the best training responses.

When planning skill development and its inclusion in a training session, the coach needs to be aware that fatigue impedes learning. Skills and tactical elements are learned faster and retained better when learning occurs in a non-fatigued state. All learning should, therefore, precede any occurrence of fatigue in a training session. To some coaches, this principle may be contradictory to their understanding of the use of the training principle of specificity. It is commonly asserted that if skills are to be performed when an athlete is tired, then learning those skills while experiencing the level of fatigue that will occur in the sporting event is the best procedure. However, techniques and tactics learned in non-fatigued states produce better performances in fatigued states than do skills that have been 'learned' in the presence of fatigue. The physiology of learning supports this contention. The formation of neuromuscular patterns is inhibited by increases in acidity of the supporting physiological environment. Thus, when lactic acid accrues as a result of fatigue, the potential for learning is reduced or even halted. Hard-line coaches consider this point of view to be sacrilege!

Structural changes that occur with fatigue also reduce the efficiency of learning. In fatigued states, the recruitment of extra muscle fibres, to support or replace those that are fatigued, produces a different neural organization from that required for an efficient performance. The nature of specific fibre recruitment has not been studied very intensively, but it does appear that patterns of recruitment are situation-dependent. The fibres that are recruited depend upon the circumstances that exist at a particular time. Hence, the pattern of movement in fatigue will vary from experience to experience.

This response variation does not increase performance efficiency. Thus it does not make sense to attempt any skill learning when athletes are in fatigued states. Attempts at learning should occur after adequate recovery from previous training-session fatigue and should precede increases in accrued fatigue in the training session. Attempts to learn skills and tactics at other times will produce less efficient, and often undesirable outcomes such as frustration or a lack of progress. Clearly, all learning experiences should be planned for the initial stages of a practice session.

The energizing forces of training are the fitness components that are stimulated. Because each component makes different physiological and neurological demands on the body, the way those components are presented in a practice session should occur in a particular order, intensity and volume. The duration of a session will depend upon the tasks presented as training stimuli, the activity forms in these tasks, the athlete's level of physical preparation for each fitness component, and the general training load.

Fatigue is the most important phenomenon that must be considered in the conduct of a training session. Psychological and fatigue states affect the learning of skills and tactics. Fatigue also inhibits the development of speed and co-ordination, and these performance components should only be trained when the muscles are rested.

KEY POINT

The hierarchy of training session activities is as follows:

1 General warm-up;
2 Learn and perfect techniques and tactics;
3 Develop speed;
4 Develop power;
5 Develop specific strength;
6 Develop muscular endurance;
7 Develop high-intensity aerobic endurance;
8 Develop low-intensity aerobic endurance;
9 Recovery routine.

A particular hierarchy for training fitness components exists, indicating that some training items must occur before others for optimal training outcomes to be produced (see Key Point, previous page). Failing to adhere to the hierarchy will reduce the potential value of a training session.

Physical Components of a Training Session

General Warm-Up

A general warm-up should initiate every session. The activities should involve all body components, with a view to increasing the temperature of the large and deep muscles. Once an adequate temperature increase is achieved, flexibility activities involving the major joints, and those joints of particular importance to swimming, should be undertaken. This order is often different from that commonly seen during swimming warm-ups. Flexibility should follow activities that make muscles warm, because warm muscles and joint structures are more flexible than cold ones and are less prone to injury. The common practice of stretching on the deck and then swimming a 'warm-up' is fundamentally wrong. It is current practice in many progressive swimming programmes for these elements to be combined as part of a 'dynamic' warm-up process on land and in the pool.

Learn and Perfect Techniques and Tactics

If learning occurs in non-fatigued states, sufficient time should be allocated to ensure that it takes place by producing desirable patterns of response. Hurried learning sessions could result in the development of more errors than desirable outcomes. Previous learning should be practised at medium and maximum intensities. Goals for execution precision should be established. Adequate recovery times between repetitions should be provided so that no performance deterioration occurs due to fatigue.

Develop Speed

Training stimuli that attempt to improve speed should be planned next. These should be of short duration (see Chapter 13) and complete recovery between each swim should be permitted. Any fatigue that exists at the start of the next repetition will reduce the specific nature of any training effect. The common practice of finishing a training session with 'sprints' is physiologically wrong because the body is usually unable to tax the capacities required for increasing speed. Speed work should occur early in, rather than at the end of, a training session.

Develop Power

Activities that require speed and strength (power) should be considered next. The rest period between each repetition will depend upon the importance of the speed factor. Interval training, which requires total recovery between repeats, is the preferred training format for this fitness component. Since the application of power is skill-dependent, obvious incursions of harmful fatigue should be avoided.

Develop Specific Strength

Within a training session, specific strength is best developed through a few maximum efforts (low repetitions with high intensity), with almost complete recovery between trials. Swimming strength is best achieved through maximum swimming efforts. It is inadvisable to attempt supplementary training (such as with weights, pulleys and so on) during or prior to a training session. Supplementary training is best scheduled after or outside of pool training sessions. Fatigue from supplementary training should not be carried into a swimming training session. Constraints such as facilities may restrict this, but every effort should be made to follow the principle.

Develop Muscular Endurance

Muscular endurance should be presented in two stages. The first bout of repetitions should comprise a moderate amount of repetitions with moderate intensity. The volume should then be increased to a higher number of repetitions with moderate resistance. The repetitions and resistances will depend upon the fitness component requirements for the event and for the individual.

Develop High-Intensity Aerobic Endurance

The first level of aerobic endurance work in the session should be the hardest. This is commonly referred to as maximum aerobic capacity, VO_2max or overload training (see Chapter 13 for more on this).

Develop Low-Intensity Aerobic Endurance

The remaining endurance work should be of a moderate intensity to initiate the winding-down of the training session.

Recovery Routine

A training session should employ a recovery or swim-down routine. The work intensity is reduced and the specific nature of activity may also be reduced. This training segment should allow athletes to leave the practice environment partly recovered and with a positive disposition, to promote interest in and enhance motivation for the next training session.

The above training sequence indicates an initial learning emphasis, an intensity peak in the middle, and an endurance dominance at the end. Not all the elements would occur in each training session, but, once selected, training segments should be ordered according to this scheme. Fig 75 illustrates a training session planning sheet that correctly orders potential training activities. When using it for writing a training session, entries should be made only alongside the activities to be performed.

In its simplest form, a training session may consist of only one segment, such as when a distance swimmer does a 10,000m timetrial. Planning which components are to be stimulated in a session depends on the requirements of the individual swimmer (see Chapter 15).

The greater the training intensity, the less will be the volume of training in a standard time period. Recovery needs increase as the intensity of training elements increase. The use of recovery periods for instruction in other domains, such as the development of psychological skills and the performance of managerial activities, should be considered to introduce increased productivity in training-time utilization. The duration of a training session is inversely proportional to the intensity of the training stimulus. Low-intensity sessions can be more time-consuming because of the large amounts of fuel stores that can be accessed and the ability of the body to maintain activity levels without incurring debilitating fatigue.

The more intense and stressful a session, the simpler its organization should be. That organization will be enhanced if the content of the session is posted and known to the swimmer before it commences. Athletes are better able to appropriate their capacities to the training segments when they know in advance what is planned. The heavier and more intense the overall load of one training session, the lighter the next session should be. Alternating training sessions in terms of volume and intensity is a sound planning principle.

The final coaching determinant of the content of a practice session is employed during the actual session. When an athlete fatigues during a session, techniques deteriorate and performances become less consistent. When technique and performance diminution occurs, it could reach a stage where any continued participation would serve no productive purpose; with extreme fatigue, the

DAY/DATE: _____	SQUAD: _____	TIME: ___
Venue:	Microcycle:	
Aim:	Objectives:	

Training Activity	Activities and Coaching Points	Intensity	Volume
1. Warm-up			
2. Technique learning			
3. Technique practice			
4. Speed			
5. Power			
6. Strength			
7. Muscular endurance			
8. Aerobic endurance high			
9. Aerobic endurance low			
10. Recovery			

Fig 75 A session-planning sheet with correctly ordered activities. (Adapted from Rushall, 1994)

consequences may even be counter-productive. Since no planning procedure for sports training is precise, coaches will have to exercise their judgement as to when a training segment should be interrupted or altered because of technique and performance deterioration.

CHAPTER 15

THE SEASON

Periodization

Two of the most common features of the training programmes of swimmers are the periodization of training, and the transition from training to racing. Periodization can be defined in simple terms as the division of the annual training plan into smaller and more manageable phases. This approach permits one aspect of fitness to be the focus of training, while maintaining the other aspects. In essence, managing a periodized training programme is really about being an organized and systematic coach.

The transition from training to racing is commonly referred to as the taper and is characterized by a reduction in the volume of training and the refinement of race speed. Both periodization and tapering lead to the peaking of performance that is necessary for competition. (Chapter 19 has more details on successful tapering for competition.)

It is a fundamental principle of preparing swimmers that periodization and tapering apply equally to all the different aspects of fitness, such as endurance, speed, strength, flexibility and power. From a physiological viewpoint, there are several reasons for a periodized and balanced training programme leading up to major competition:

- avoiding a high training load with excessive fatigue;
- faster recovery and regeneration;
- maintaining performances very close to their maximum for a long period of time;
- correct peaking for the major competition of the year;
- maintaining a basic level of fitness over a long period of training (or even a period of reduced training);

- a greater degree of specificity to be incorporated in training;
- a more efficient and effective taper;
- more complete adaptation to training without two or three parts of the programme interfering with each other when trained concurrently;
- better planning for both major and minor competitions;
- more effective integration of sports-science testing with the training programme.

A periodized swimming training and tapering programme is based on the principle of overload–recovery–peaking. This principle forms the basis of the preparation of swimming training programmes with the aim of increasing the level of competitive performance. The training programme must provide an overload (stimulus), to force the body to adapt to a previously un-encountered level of stress. After sufficient application of the stimulus (in terms of magnitude and frequency), a period of recovery and regeneration will allow residual fatigue to dissipate. If the processes of overload and recovery are managed correctly (in other words, if there is effective periodization), a period of super-compensation will occur so that performance is elevated to a higher level for important competitions.

> **KEY POINT**
>
> The most important consideration is that peaking for performance is an active process. Put as much effort into the planning and execution of the tapering and peaking programme as you put into regular training.

Cycles

Most swimming coaches are familiar with the term 'periodization' and the various macro-, meso- and microcycles that are employed in designing a training programme. These terms are used to establish a sequencing of training within the overall programme.

Macrocycle

A 'macrocycle' refers to a long-term training phase lasting several weeks to months. In swimming, this usually represents the entire season in preparation for a major, annual competition. Most commonly, there is a two-peak year, with emphasis first on the national swimming championships and then on the major international competition, such as the Olympics or World Championships, held later in the year. The precise length of the macrocycle will depend on the specific training and/or competition objectives for the season and the current fitness level of the individual swimmer.

> **KEY POINT**
>
> The annual plan and the competition calendar are essential tools. To achieve extraordinary results you need an extraordinarily good training programme. At best, last year's programme may bring you last year's results.

Mesocycle

The term 'mesocycle' refers to shorter training blocks within the macrocycle. Typically, these are anything from seven to twenty weeks in length. A number of mesocycles combine to form a single phase of training, for example, the preparatory phase. Experience and scientific research have shown that, after several weeks of intensive training, most athletes require some period of recovery. Hence the 'cyclical' nature of training over extended periods of time.

There are many types of mesocycle, depending on the requirements of the programme, coach and swimmer. Some examples used by swimming coaches are the introductory cycle (general training, low-volume, low-intensity), preparatory cycle (transition from low-volume, low-intensity to higher-volume training), specific cycle (more specialized higher-intensity training, with emphasis on improving competitive speed) and the competition cycle (competitive performance on a single or repeated basis). In each case, the volume and intensity of work will vary according to the specific requirements of the programme for the swimmers. Effective coaches are always aware of 'where they are' in the training programme. Getting bogged down and stale in a long and arduous training phase is not a very efficient approach to preparing for competition. Athletes should not struggle with their training for more than a few days without some intervention, otherwise over-training may occur.

KEY POINT

Swimmers should be able to train close to race speed when required. This is achieved by the careful management of endurance, speed and recovery.

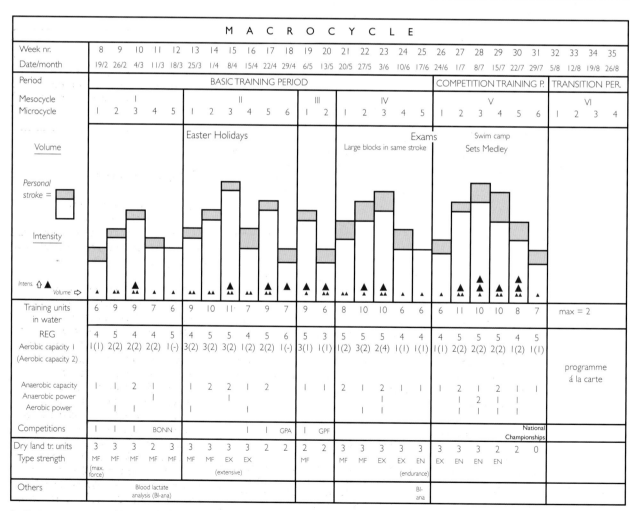

Fig 76 An annual macrocycle.

Microcycle

The term 'microcycle' refers to a short-term training block within a mesocycle. Most commonly, swimming training microcycles are planned around a standard seven-day training week. Most swimmers have to fit their training programme around work, education and family commitments. However, coming in to important meets such as the Olympics, the training schedule takes precedence, and the day of the week, weekends and public holidays become less important.

Microcycles represent the specific plans and strategies needed to achieve the broader objective of the training cycle, for example, improving anaerobic capacity. Each microcycle consists of the individual (daily) workouts and again these are based on the objectives of the mesocycle.

KEY POINT

Coaches and swimmers should plan broad details for a mesocycle, specific details for a microcycle, and fine-tune training details on a daily basis.

Planning Cycles

In most swimming programmes across the world, one of the fundamental principles of the periodization of training is that volume of training is increased before intensity of training. Most coaches are familiar with the concept that a foundation of aerobic fitness is established easily in the cycle or competition season. After this initial period of increasing training volume to build endurance, the emphasis of training switches to the development of speed and anaerobic capacities. It is often observed that this base level of fitness can be re-established fairly quickly (in four to six weeks) in those swimmers with an extensive training background. This has implications for more mature swimmers who are returning after a break. However, it is much more efficient for swimmers to

maintain a basic fitness programme during the off-season. A reasonable level of fitness can be maintained on about 30 per cent of the full training volume, so a swimmer who normally undertakes ten training sessions a week should be able to maintain a base level of fitness for several weeks by training three times per week. In this case, it is important to maintain some intensity in the work as volume and duration are reduced.

KEY POINT

Although the requirement for aerobic work applies mainly to the middle-distance and distance events, the shorter sprint events may also benefit from this type of training for general conditioning and recovery purposes.

The principle of volume first, intensity second is valuable in terms of designing microcycles. One approach that is successful in certain situations is the use of three-day microcycles. The first variant involves two training sessions a day for the first two days, followed by a single session on the third day. In some circumstances in swimming, where three training sessions a day are used, the second variation takes the form of three sessions a day for two days, and then two sessions on the third and final day. In both versions, the first day is largely aerobic in nature, with a gradual decrease in volume and increase in intensity as the microcycle proceeds. The emphasis is on increasing speed from day to day, and athletes generally find this easier if the training volume is decreasing. Many swimmers (and coaches) like to finish each microcycle with a quality or speed session.

KEY POINT

The swimming coach should be proactive: making and dictating the move from volume to intensity, endurance to speed and training to racing.

Another feature of training planning is the relationship between duration and intensity. Generally speaking, the lower the intensity of the cycle, the longer its duration. For higher-intensity work, shorter, two- to four-day training cycles are used. Variation of training distance and intensity within cycles is important. Early in the programme, microcycles may involve higher-intensity training for swimmers who are already fatigued. The thinking is that this will provide a greater stimulus for adaptation. Later on, when the emphasis is on competition-specific speed, it is usually better to undertake high-intensity training in a fresh condition in order to facilitate higher speeds.

KEY POINT

When peaking, the development of race speed should take priority over conditioning work in the pool or gym.

A Typical Mesocycle

A typical fifteen-week swimming preparation between national championships and the major international meet may encompass some or all of the following features.

Cycle 1: Aerobic (Weeks 1–5)
As in most training programmes, the initial phase involves the development or re-establishment of endurance fitness. This acts as a basis for the subsequent development of aerobic and anaerobic capacities and, importantly, the functional utilization of these capacities. Apart from the underlying physiological adaptations, improved endurance will lead to an increased ability to cope with fatigue and more rapid recovery from the stresses of speed training and competition. In particular, the aim is to develop the capacity and efficiency of the aerobic or cardio-respiratory system. This process is largely achieved by high-volume, low-intensity training.

Other adaptations with this kind of training include increased utilization of fat as a fuel source, stronger ligaments, tendons and connective tissue, changes within slow-twitch muscle fibres, and improved neuromuscular control. The length of this phase will depend on several factors – the fitness level of the swimmers, the time available, and the objectives of the cycle – but they normally last for three to five weeks.

KEY POINT

Control the intensity of training by speed (pacing), heart rate and perception of effort (by the athlete) – do not neglect any one factor.

Cycle 2: Aerobic/Anaerobic (Weeks 6–9)

In this cycle, the other primary components of aerobic training are developed. Assuming that low- to moderate-intensity endurance work is developed in the first cycle, this cycle is characterized by an emphasis on anaerobic threshold training. For example, swimmers may undertake up to 30 per cent of work in this cycle at the level of anaerobic threshold, and up to 15 per cent of maximal oxygen uptake and lactate-tolerance work. The levels will vary for different events. The total training volume

is increased over Cycle 1 and there is a progressive introduction of shorter and faster intervals. The duration of the cycle is normally three to four weeks.

Cycle 3: Transition (Weeks 10–12)

In many ways, this is the key training phase. The aim is to develop the functional utilization of the energy systems and capacities that were developed in the aerobic endurance and aerobic/anaerobic cycles. It is well documented that the factor that correlates most highly with endurance performance is the speed at anaerobic threshold. This important point is often overlooked, but Swimmer A is likely to perform better if his speed is faster than Swimmer B at the same relative anaerobic threshold. Improvement of the functional utilization (speed at a given metabolic load) is achieved through training sets of higher intensity but shorter duration, at speeds close to and faster than competitive speeds. The high degree of aerobic fitness developed earlier will be maintained, even though the emphasis of training is on higher-quality intervals. This cycle is fairly short with an average length of two to three weeks.

KEY POINT

Use speed-assisted drills: group work or pace work with similar or faster swimmers.

Cycle 4: Taper and Competition (Weeks 13–15)

The final cycle within this phase of the season involves the tapering period and the competition peak. Again, the logic follows the preceding cycles and training is characterized by a further reduction in training volume, and the development of speed and power. In swimming, it is common to reduce the training volume by approximately a half to two-thirds of the peak weekly volume. The key is to reduce the volume and sharpen the speed; for example, for 100m swimmers, there would be an emphasis on 25m and 50m intervals at faster than 100m race pace. It is important to maintain some aerobic training in this cycle and a common mistake is to reduce training mileage too rapidly. Aerobic work is needed to support the taper and forms an essential part of the recovery and regeneration process prior to competition.

KEY POINT

Peaking is an active process of training and is achieved by a well-planned and executed training and recovery programme.

CHAPTER 16

NUTRITION

The body requires energy for every physical activity, and the amount it needs depends on the duration and type of activity. Energy is measured in kcal and is obtained from the body stores or food consumed. Glycogen is the main source of fuel used by the muscles to enable the body to undertake both aerobic and anaerobic exercise. A swimmer who trains with low glycogen stores will feel constantly tired, his training performance will be diminished and he will be more prone to injury and illness.

KEY POINT

A calorie (cal) is the amount of heat energy required to raise the temperature of 1g of water 1°C, from 14 to 15°C. A kilocalorie (kcal) is the amount of heat required to raise the temperature of 1,000g of water 1°C.

Nutrient Balance

Carefully planned nutrition must provide an energy balance, and the diet should comprise a combination of the following nutrients:

- proteins: essential to growth and repair of muscle and other body tissues;
- fats: one source of energy and important in relation to fat-soluble vitamins;
- carbohydrates: the body's main source of energy;
- minerals: those inorganic elements occurring in the body that are critical to its normal functions;

- vitamins: water- and fat-soluble vitamins play an important role in many chemical processes in the body;
- water: essential to normal body function, both as a vehicle for carrying other nutrients and because 60 per cent of the human body is water;
- roughage: the fibrous indigestible portion of the diet that is essential to the health of the digestive system.

Nutrition for Energy

The energy needed by the body has to be blended. The blend required by competitive swimmers is as follows:

- 65–75 per cent carbohydrates (sugar, sweets, bread, cakes);
- 15–25 per cent fats (dairy products, oil);
- 10–15 per cent protein (eggs, milk, meat, poultry, fish).

Carbohydrates

There are two types of carbohydrate: starchy (complex) carbohydrates and simple sugars. The simple sugars are found in confectionery, muesli bars, cakes and biscuits, cereals, puddings, soft drinks and juices, and jam and honey, but these food stuffs also contain fat. Starchy carbohydrates are found in potatoes, rice, bread, wholegrain cereals, semi-skimmed milk, yoghurt, fruit, vegetables, beans and pulses. Both types effectively replace muscle glycogen. The starchy carbohydrates are the ones that have all the vitamins and minerals in them as well as protein. They are also low in fat, as long as they are not served up with loads of butter and fatty sauces. The starchy foods are much more

---

MEASURING ENERGY

Energy expended and consumed is measured in kilocalories (kcal) or kilojoules (kJ). The amount of energy gained from 1g of pure carbohydrate, fat or protein is as follows:

1g of carbohydrate	4kcl
1g of fat	9kcal
1g of protein	4kcal

It is possible to obtain the overall energy value of different foods if you know what quantities are present. Nowadays, this information is frequently written on the packaging and it is therefore possible to work out what percentage of energy is being supplied by each of the three nutrients.

Let us compare the contents of 100g of a chocolate wafer bar and 100g of a shredded wheat breakfast cereal. The percentage of energy gained from the nutrients in the chocolate bar are: carbohydrates 47 per cent, fats 47 per cent, protein 6 per cent. The percentage of energy gained from the nutrients in the shredded wheat are: carbohydrates 81 per cent, fats 6 per cent, protein 13 per cent. Therefore, of the two examples, the complex carbohydrate shredded wheat is by far the healthier option.

---

bulky so there can be a problem in eating a sufficiently large amount of food; supplementing them with simple sugar alternatives may be necessary.

The digestive system converts the carbohydrates in food into glucose, a form of sugar carried in the blood and transported to cells for energy. The glucose, in turn, is broken down into carbon dioxide and water. Any glucose not used by the cells is converted into glycogen – another form of carbohydrate that is stored in the muscles and liver. However, the body's glycogen capacity is limited to about 350g; once this maximum has been reached, any excess glucose is quickly converted into fat.

A main meal should be based upon a bulk of carbohydrates and small amounts of protein such as meat, poultry and fish. The extra protein and vitamins needed will be in the starchy carbohydrates.

Following training and competition, a swimmer's glycogen stores are depleted. In order to replenish them, the swimmer needs to consider the speed at which carbohydrate is converted into blood glucose and transported to the muscles. The rapid replenishment of glycogen stores is important for the swimmer who has a number of races in a meet. The rise in blood glucose levels is indicated by a food's glycaemic index (GI); the faster and higher the rise in blood glucose, the higher the GI. Studies have shown that consuming high-GI carbohydrates (approximately 1g per kg body weight) within two hours of finishing exercise speeds up the replenishment of glycogen stores, and therefore speeds up recovery time. There are times when it is beneficial to consume lower-GI carbohydrates, which are absorbed slowly over a longer period of time (two to four hours before exercise). Eating five or six meals or snacks a day will help maximize glycogen stores and energy levels, minimize fat storage and stabilize blood glucose and insulin levels.

Fats

The nature of fats depends on the type of fatty acids that make up the triglycerides. All fats contain both saturated and unsaturated fatty acids, but they are usually described as 'saturated' or 'unsaturated' according to the proportion of fatty acids present. As a rough guide, saturated fats are generally solid at room temperature and tend to be animal fats. Unsaturated fats are liquid at room temperature and are usually vegetable fats, although there are exceptions – palm oil is a vegetable oil that contains a high percentage of saturated fatty acids.

Eating and Drinking Before, During and After Competition

What you eat on a day-to-day basis is extremely important for training. Your diet will affect how fast and how well you progress, and how soon you reach competitive standard. Once you are ready to compete, you will have a new concern: your competition diet. Is it important? What should you eat before your competition? When is the best time to eat? How much should you eat? Should you be eating during the event? And what can you eat between heats? A lot of research has been done in this area, and it is clear that certain dietary approaches can enhance competition performance.

Monitor your daily intake (especially your carbohydrates) and then adjust your diet to meet your daily requirements. A good, balanced diet should provide you with the required nutrients but it does need to be monitored. The simplest way to monitor the 'energy balance' is to keep a regular check of your weight.

Hydration and Supplements

Swimmers should be well hydrated before beginning exercise; they should also drink enough fluid during and after exercise to balance fluid losses. During exercise, sports drinks containing carbohydrates and electrolytes will provide fuel for the muscles, help maintain blood-glucose levels and the thirst mechanism, and decrease the risk of dehydration.

Swimmers will not need vitamin and mineral supplements if adequate energy to maintain body weight is consumed from a variety of foods. However, supplements may be required by athletes who restrict energy intake, have severe weight-loss practices, or eliminate one or more food groups from their diet. Nutritional, ergogenic aids should be used with caution, and only after careful evaluation of the product for safety, for efficacy, for potency, and to determine whether or not it is a banned or illegal substance.

Pre-Competition

In the week leading up to the event:

- ensure a high-carbohydrate eating plan;
- include more rice and pasta: they have more carbohydrate than potato;
- include nutritious carbohydrate-based between-meal snacks (see below);
- as your training will be tapered pre-event, you will not need to eat more;
- eating the right balance of increased carbohydrate and less fat is the key.

At the Competition

Consider the following guidelines relating to the pre-event meal:

- eat it about two to three hours before competition (approximately two to three hours before warm-up);
- it should top up blood-sugar levels after the night's rest;
- it does not have to be large, but should fill you up for the next few hours;
- high-carbohydrate foods – bread, cereals, fruit, pasta, rice, and so on – are the best options;
- ensure it is low in fat, as this speeds up digestion;
- eat breakfast before getting to the pool, as this leaves time for the carbo fuel to get in;
- have a drink – sports drink, juice, or a liquid meal – to optimize hydration; avoid cola drinks, coffee, chocolate and tea, as the caffeine in them is dehydrating;
- if you feel too nervous to eat, try a liquid meal (see below);
- practise with your pre-event meal prior to nationals to fine-tune this eating strategy.

After the warm-up, the swimmer needs to recover for the heats:

- replace fluids immediately (leave your drink bottle at pool side); sports drinks are optimal, as they replace fluids and carbohydrate simultaneously;
- if there is less than one hour between races, replace fluids only; if there is

more than one hour to wait, try to eat a little (see 'top-up between event' ideas, below).

Generally, the best approach is to eat a little and often during the day, and to seize the opportunity to 'top up' whenever possible. This approach will help to keep you 'firing' all day and prevent you getting really hungry. Eating too much at once can make you feel heavy and lethargic.

The following guidelines should be considered in relation to drinking and eating between events:

- try to eat in longer breaks (longer than one hour between races);
- in shorter breaks, use a sports drink or water to replace fluids;
- if there is a longer break (a few hours) through the day, use it to eat a bit more;
- remember that the indoor pool environment is humid and dehydrating, and adequate fluids are essential all day to keep the blood and energy pumping;
- take your own high-performance foods and drinks with you (do not rely on the canteen); a cold pack and thermos will

help to keep foods and drinks fresh;
- record food and fluid intakes;
- monitor hydration by checking that urine output is regular and looks 'clear'; monitoring body-weight change over the day is another way to check hydration.

It is essential to initiate the body's recovery as soon as possible after a hard day's competition, by doing the following:

- have something to drink and eat immediately after your last swim;
- avoid the 'fast food' chains on the way home – their high-fat foods will delay recovery;
- have some high-carbohydrate food ready-prepared, so you can eat as soon as you arrive home;
- if possible, take a thermos with a meal in it to the competition, so you can eat even earlier;
- check your body weight to ensure that you are re-hydrated.

COMPETITION-DAY NUTRITION

Top-up snacks between events (during breaks of one to two hours):
- snack fruits (small cans of fruit) or canned fruits designed for babies;
- bananas;
- fruit that is peeled and cut up (easier to eat this way);
- plain bread rolls (white bread may be less heavy), or pitta bread;
- fruit buns (for example, hot cross buns) or raisin bread;
- plain or fruit scones;
- home-made low-fat fruit muffins;
- rice cakes (topped with honey, jam or banana);
- boiled or milky or creamed rice (use reduced-fat milk);
- rice pudding or bread pudding (use reduced-fat milk);
- jam or honey sandwiches;

- plain boiled pasta with a little tomato sauce;
- low-fat breakfast or plain muesli bar;
- fruit fingers (see baby food selection at the supermarket);
- plain crackers (not high-fat types);
- small amount of reduced-fat yoghurt;
- carbohydrate gels;
- power bars (or equivalent).

Best fluid replacers over the day:
- sports drink (contains carbohydrate to boost energy as well);
- water.

In longer breaks or after the competition:
- sandwiches with low-fat fillings (avoid butter and too much salad);
- pasta or rice with tomato pasta sauce (a little chicken or very lean meat in sauce is OK).

STAR TIP

Practise with all eating and drinking strategies prior to the championships to fine-tune the plan for the competition. Everyone is different and various combinations of the above, tailored to your individual needs, will work best.

PART 4

COMPETITION

CHAPTER 17

COMPETITION PSYCHOLOGY

The major emphasis of competitive swimming is competing. Through competitions, swimmers are subjected to the responsibility of doing their best in a public forum. The consequences of such performances are very intense, primarily because of expectations and the number of people (teammates, parents, relatives, coaches) who witness the swimmer's efforts. For this reason, young and inexperienced swimmers have to like competing if they are to enjoy the sport fully. It is usual for inexperienced swimmers to develop their attitudes towards competing through trial-and-error experiences and quite often with less than adequate direction from a coach. Often, they are subjected to conflicting instructions when teammates, parents and the coach all give 'helpful' advice.

The following tips (below) should act as imperatives rather than aspirations for swimmers, coaches, parents, officials and so on:

Pre-race and race strategies feature strongly in the psychological preparation programmes of coaches and swimmers. In order to be fully effective they need to adhere to certain key features. Fig 77 (opposite) shows a hierarchy of psychological interventions for use in swimming. The rest of this chapter highlights five areas of behavioural psychology that swimmers and coaches can use to improve performance:

1 Positive thinking;
2 Content decision-making;
3 Self-fulfilling prophecy;
4 Coping skills; and
5 Segmenting strategies.

Positive Thinking

Negative orientations are detrimental to competitive performances. Examples of negative orientations are worry, wishing you did not have to race, racing not to let others down, and trying to avoid a bad performance. Negative approaches produce a physiological reaction that is different from the reaction that occurs under a positive attitude. Swimmers function less efficiently, fatigue more easily, and use different physiological ingredients in their exercise response than when they are positive. Less work is performed under a negative 'mind-set' than under a positive one.

Swimmers need to interpret every racing situation so that the purpose of competing is to achieve positive outcomes. After a race, a swimmer should focus on and emphasize what was done well. If losing is likely, then winning should not be a goal. Other performance goals should be established, such as improving technique, improved pacing, consistent split times, or setting a personal best (PB). With a positive approach to racing, a swimmer will strive to do things well in every race. Performance expectations that have a high degree of negative potential

---

TIPS FOR COMPETING

- competitions should only be interpreted as a positive experience;
- in early competitions, the focus should be on reproducing in races what has been done in training;
- competition content of junior swimmers should be determined by the training effects that have been consistently demonstrated in practice;
- stressing in competitions only those factors that can be controlled by the athlete is a performance principle that transcends all levels of competitions and experience;
- swimmers should always look for what is done well and what can be improved as a way of maintaining a positive orientation to competing;

- a lack of improvement in competition may indicate a failure of the training programme to influence competitive performance;
- swimmers should be taught how to handle disruptive events at competitions;
- if competing is initially an unpleasant experience for a new swimmer, that swimmer may develop a dislike of competing or may interpret the experience negatively;
- the coach should model appropriate behaviours at competitions;
- the goals of competing should be many rather than few;
- events or procedures that have not been practised successfully and consistently should not be attempted at competitions;
- vague goals increase uncertainty and increase the probability of misinterpretation;

- swimmers should be taught to use post-race behaviours and events to maximize the 'experience' potential of racing;
- the primary focus of goal-setting should be to achieve performance characteristics over which the swimmer has control;
- racing goals should be established by the athlete and coach as a collaborative activity;
- the planning and organization around competitions that is controlled by the coach should aim to reduce the level of stress for the athlete;
- self-talk focusing on the goals of the race assists swimmers to stay on task;
- racing should be viewed as an opportunity to demonstrate to new athletes their improvements and progress in the sport.

should be ignored or eliminated. The goal-package must be positive so that an athlete races to achieve things or improve in performance factors.

A swimmer should look forward to testing himself to gain something from a race. Those gains should be trained for, achievable, and/or indicate improvement. A

KEY POINT

The fruits of training are more likely to be achieved through a positive attitude.

---

positive approach to racing will result in a swimmer exploiting the best physiology that training has led him to achieve. The amount of negative thought content prior to and during a race determines a major portion of performance deterioration. If you think badly, you will perform badly.

Content Decision-Making

Performance outcomes are more likely to be achieved when what is to be done prior to and during a race has been planned,

practised, and shown to be successful. New approaches, techniques or strategies should never be used in races without having been tested, refined and trained. A swimmer should prepare for and race with what is known and has been practised.

If thinking while performing is practised, swimmers can learn to think clearly in a race. Combining thought practice with physical training allows the skill of thought control to develop and to be used in a race. Mental functioning needs to be trained in physically stressful conditions. At all times at practice and in races, a swimmer should maintain mental control.

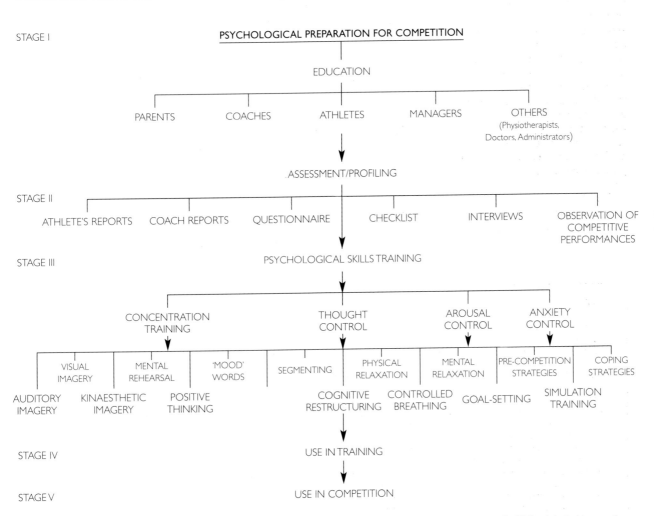

Fig 77 Psychological interventions.

Much effort is needed in the initial stages of developing this capacity.

If a swimmer has the responsibility for the major portion of the decision-making when structuring strategy content, an enhanced approach to racing will result. Strategies must be specific in content and extreme in detail. This athlete-centred approach to racing will have the following effects upon performance:

- uncertainty and interpretive distractions are reduced;
- the stressfulness of negative situations is reduced;
- performance consistency is produced;
- the coping capacity for problem situations is enhanced; and
- performance drop-offs are minimized.

> **KEY POINT**
>
> When swimmers are given the major responsibility for planning and deciding on what is to be included in strategies, performances are enhanced. Coaches and parents should resist telling swimmers what they want them to do in races and let those decisions be made by the athletes.

Self-Fulfilling Prophecy

Swimmers who believe they have little chance of achieving goals or being successful are likely to perform at a low level. When an individual predicts a negative outcome, that outcome is very likely to be the result. (This theory does not, however, work in reverse, for positive predictions; that is, if an individual predicts success, success does not necessarily ensue.)

Negative approaches to racing can be discerned by listening to what a swimmer says. Positive statements, such as 'I am able to perform my best', 'I will set the race tempo' and 'I am going to pace the whole race evenly', indicate assertiveness and confidence, features of a positive approach to racing. On the other hand, statements such as 'I hope I can do well', 'I think I can put on a good show' and 'I pray I will not let anyone down', indicate uncertainty about, or reliance on an external entity for, performance. To avoid negative self-fulfilling prophecies, swimmers have to develop positive predictions, justifications and expectations prior to races. They should know what they want to do, how they will do it, and then go ahead and do it.

Thinking of trying to avoid falling behind in a race is an avoidance orientation that will promote reduced physiological and skill efficiency. Rather, a swimmer should think of the technique items that will produce the best, sustainable, steady-state swimming, actions that will result in a competent response to the task. This latter description is a positive approach to the same problem. Its effect will not depreciate a performance; it is more likely to enhance it.

> **KEY POINT**
>
> Thinking of errors, possible weaknesses or failures, or potential problems, before or during a race, will increase the likelihood of them occurring.

Coping Skills

The inclusion of coping skills in pre-race and race planning is essential. Their practice and emphasis should consume about 20 per cent of training time. Coping behaviours should not be confused with negative thinking. Predicting and preparing for problems – that is, knowing what to do if something goes wrong – will produce better tolerance and coping responses prior to and in a race. In most cases, problems are handled and the swimmer 'gets back on track' with performing the planned strategy and achieving goals. Successful coping in problem circumstances produces a positive orientation. Normally, problems lead to negative orientations if a coping response is not attempted.

Swimmers should practise and learn to cope with problems through worst-case simulations. A very simple example of a coping strategy adopted by most swimmers is to carry a spare set of goggles when reporting for a race.

> **KEY POINT**
>
> For every preferred action to be performed and thought of prior to or during a race there should be an alternative fallback action that is another way of achieving the same intended outcome. Coping positively maintains performance capacity. A failure to cope reduces performance capacity.

Segmenting Strategies

Breaking a race down into meaningful sections of skills, terrain and thought control is called 'segmenting'. Each segment should have its own set of goals. A preparation or performance becomes the task of serially achieving the goals of each segment. Focusing on the intermediate goals of segments influences performance maximally. For example, what a swimmer wants to achieve as the final outcome of a 1,500m may have very little to do with the first two minutes of swimming in that race. On the other hand, if a strategy has been developed that requires certain things to be done to achieve a very good start, and establish pace and rhythm, and that is what is focused on in the first two minutes of the race, that short-term concentration may affect performance positively.

> **KEY POINT**
>
> Pre-race strategies should be structured in sequential segments. The successful completion of each activity will signal 'good' preparations and will develop a positive mind-set.

Segmented races require thinking of the race stage of the moment. The attainment of final goals is dependent upon correctly completing all the segments that lead to the finish. Thinking of the final goal other than in the final segment is a disruptive pursuit that will cause performance to be reduced. Concentrating on achieving segment goals, in the order in which they are planned, produces sustained performances. A swimmer should only think of what is needed to achieve the segment goals at each stage of a race. The aim of racing under this format is to achieve successive goals according to the planned strategy and race stage. If segment goals are not achieved, coping procedures are required at the start of the next segment to help the swimmer recover positive and planned control.

The transition stage from one segment to the next is a unique feature of pre-race and race strategies. At the end of a segment the following sequence of events should occur:

- evaluate very quickly whether or not the goals of the segment have been achieved;
- proceed with the execution of the next segment if the goals have been achieved;
- in the case of failure to achieve the goals of the previous segment, enact a recovery routine that will correct the reasons for that failure;
- enter the next segment strategy at the appropriate stage as soon as recovery procedures are completed.

Segmenting a performance means that a swimmer will know what is to be done in order to achieve final preparation and competition goals. The frequent attainment of segment goals maintains a positive approach to performance and enhances a swimmer's momentum to perform. The segmentation of strategies produces many desirable effects that enhance achievements and consistency. Swimmers and coaches should practise this approach throughout the season, building up to the main competition peak.

Summary

Maintenance of a positive mind-set during a race directly enhances the type and efficiency of physiological reactions to a performance. Racing without a positive orientation results in an inferior level of performance. Preparing all or the major portion of strategies produces heightened performances. The prediction of problems reduces performance because of the phenomenon of the self-fulfilling prophecy. However, the development of coping skills for potential problems will reduce the effect of preparatory and in-race problems, should they occur. A considerable amount of training time should be devoted to practising coping responses. A segmented preparation and race will produce better performances than when all activities are oriented towards some set of final goals. Segmenting a strategy makes it more controllable and increases performance application and consistency. These factors need to be considered when pre-race and race strategies are developed.

CHAPTER 18

COMPETITION ANALYSIS

The evaluation of race strategy beyond basic split times (splits) has been of interest to coaches for as long as athletes have been swimming. However, it was really only in the early 1970s that researchers and coaches expanded their analysis to include more variables than splits. Many techniques have been developed to offer scientists a method for comparing elite swimmers to average swimmers, and to allow coaches a better method of evaluating the strengths and weaknesses of a swimmer's performances. 'Race Analysis' is now commonly used across the world to assess competition performance.

The primary objectives in the continued development of race-analysis systems are the following:

- the collection of information that coaches and swimmers use every day to evaluate and improve performance;
- the creation of accurate and easy-to-use measurement tools; and
- the organization of information for long-term athlete comparison (meet to meet, or year to year).

Data Collected

The protocols for race-analysis systems vary according to the development process in each country, but the basic components are common to all. Information is collected by means of fixed video cameras and processed by a software package to produce the basic performance data. The information measured during a race includes the following variables:

1 Breakout time: the time from starting signal (start) or feet leaving the wall (turns), to head breaking the surface.

2 Breakout distance: the distance from the wall where a swimmer's head breaks the surface, in metres.
3 Split: official subtractive split time for the distance measured (usually 50m).
4 Drop-off: the difference in seconds between the distance measured and the preceding distance, for example, first and second 50m of 100m race.
5 Cycle count: number of stroke cycles during the lap (one cycle = one arm stroke for fly and breaststroke and one cycle = two arm strokes for back and free).
6 Time: official cumulative time in the race.
7 Tempo/rate: frequency of swimming cycles during the lap measured. Expressed in both cycles per minute, and seconds per cycle.
8 DPC ('Distance per Cycle'): metres covered during one stroke cycle during the length measured.

9 Velocity: swimming velocity in metres/second during the free-swimming portion of the length measured, in other words, without the start or turns.
10 Turn time: time in seconds to execute each turn, usually measured no more than 5m in and up to 10m out from the wall.
11 15m start: time in seconds from starting tone to the 15m mark.
12 15m velocity: average velocity over first 15m of race.
13 7.5m finish: time in seconds from 7.5m remaining in race to finish.
14 7.5m velocity: average velocity over last 7.5m of the race.

Swimmers are tracked during the heats and the information provided to their coaches before the finals session in the evening at most major competitions.

The Constituent Parts of the Swimmer's Result

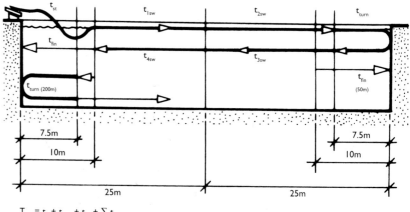

$$T_{100} = t_{st} + t_{turn} + t_{fin} + \Sigma\, t_{sw}$$

Fig 78 Race analysis set-up.

Fig 79 gives an example of the kind of information provided by the race-analysis system used at the 2003 World Championships.

Data Analysis

As an example the 1999 Pan Pacific Swimming Championship race analysis data indicates that the relationship between the quality of swimming performance and stroke length was not as significant as is commonly assumed. The average 'clean swimming' speed was significantly correlated to race results for all events as expected. The next most highly correlated variable with race performance was the turn time, which was significant in 92 per cent of all events. Start and turn times along with clean swimming speed were considered significant in butterfly, backstroke and breaststroke. This was similar to the freestyle events but these races also showed that the finish time was an important part of obtaining a good race result. The second half of the race was more strongly related to race performance than the first half of the distance races in all events except for the women's 400m Freestyle. In the individual medley events, turn performance was significantly related to race performance. It was also found that the most significant individual stroke within the medley races was breaststroke, followed by backstroke, butterfly and freestyle.

This information is considered accurate for elite-level swimmers and can be used to develop a general competition model. Individual swimmers and coaches should work on appropriate race and training strategies to suit their own strengths and weaknesses.

Stroke Rates and Lengths

The most common form of competition analysis in use today by coaches is the measurement of stroke rates and stroke lengths. Without using sophisticated

						SWIMMING STROKE AVERAGES					
Swimmer	Country	Lane	Time	Average Event Velocity (m/s)	Start Speed 15m (m/s)	Velocity (m/s)	Frequency (c/min)	Str. L (m/c)	Str. Index (m/s × m/c)	TURN (15m) Mean Speed (m/s)	Finish (5m) Mean Speed (m/s)
KITAJIMA	JPN	4	2:09.42	1.55	2.18	1.47	38	2.37	3.50	1.68	1.32
EDMOND	GBR	5	2:10.92	1.53	2.16	1.44	35	2.49	3.60	1.67	1.41
HANSEN	USA	3	2:11.11	1.53	2.12	1.46	41	2.12	3.10	1.63	1.28
PIPER	AUS	6	2:11.55	1.52	2.25	1.44	37	2.32	3.35	1.65	1.36
KOMORNIKOV	RUS	2	2:12.30	1.51	2.23	1.45	42	2.07	2.97	1.58	1.33
IVANOV	RUS	7	2:13.20	1.50	2.03	1.43	38	2.27	3.24	1.61	1.39
BROWN	CAN	8	2:13.30	1.50	2.04	1.43	35	2.49	3.55	1.60	1.36
PODOPRIGORA	AUT	1	2:13.33	1.50	2.09	1.45	43	1.99	2.87	1.55	1.32
		Average	2:11.89	1.52	2.14	1.44	39	2.27	3.27	1.62	1.35

	Kitajima	Edmond	Hansen	Piper	Komornikov	Ivanov	Brown	Podoprigora
0–15	0:06.88	0:06.96	0:07.08	0:06.68	0:06.72	0:07.40	0:07.36	0:07.16
15–25	0:06.28	0:06.60	0:06.28	0:06.60	0:06.44	0:06.64	0:06.72	0:06.48
25–42.5	0:11.52	0:11.76	0:11.40	0:11.84	0:11.52	0:11.60	0:12.04	0:11.76
57.5–75	0:12.12	0:12.28	0:12.04	0:12.32	0:12.12	0:12.56	0:12.28	0:12.12
75–92.5	0:11.84	0:12.00	0:11.76	0:11.96	0:12.44	0:12.00	0:12.12	0:12.32
107.5–125	0:12.20	0:12.20	0:12.20	0:12.36	0:11.96	0:12.64	0:12.28	0:11.92
125–142.5	0:12.04	0:12.00	0:12.24	0:12.28	0:12.44	0:12.36	0:12.32	0:12.44
157.5–175	0:12.32	0:12.64	0:12.16	0:12.60	0:12.40	0:12.40	0:12.48	0:12.40
175–195	0:14.00	0:14.40	0:14.76	0:14.36	0:14.44	0:14.36	0:14.28	0:14.20
last 5	0:03.42	0:03.20	0:03.51	0:03.31	0:03.38	0:03.24	0:03.30	0:03.41
turn 50	0:08.76	0:08.92	0:08.80	0:08.84	0:09.08	0:08.88	0:09.28	0:09.40
turn 100	0:08.96	0:08.92	0:09.12	0:09.04	0:09.48	0:09.48	0:09.28	0:09.84
turn 150	0:09.08	0:09.04	0:09.76	0:09.36	0:09.88	0:09.64	0:09.56	0:09.88
time-50	0:29.46	0:30.39	0:29.48	0:29.89	0:29.61	0:30.48	0:31.18	0:30.27
time-100	1:02.47	1:03.51	1:02.35	1:03.12	1:03.61	1:04.16	1:04.81	1:04.43
time-150	1:35.75	1:36.80	1:36.02	1:37.03	1:37.57	1:38.73	1:39.07	1:38.73

Fig 79 Example of race analysis data.

equipment (most stopwatches have an in-built stroke-rate function), instant information about stroke efficiency can be obtained. This can be used in competition and training and is applicable from early competitive levels through to international events. Stroke rate is usually given as cycles per minute, but seconds per stroke or strokes per second can also be easily calculated. The simplest stroke length measure is to count the number of stroke cycles per lap. Fig 80 shows the range of stroke rates and stroke lengths for international swimmers in each competitive event. These data were collected by the author from personal attendance at major championships and from worldwide scientific studies conducted since 1996.

A useful training tool in the development of appropriate stroke rates is the innovative 'AQUAPACER' audio signal device. No longer than a key fob, it is placed in the swimmer's cap and emits an audible pulse. It is the brainchild of Scottish coach, Patrick Miley, and has revolutionized coaching practice and made it so much easier to individually programme training sets at competition stroke rates.

EVENTS	STROKE RATES IN CYCLES/MIN	STROKE LENGTHS IN M/CYCLE
WOMEN		
50 freestyle	60–65	1.79–1.96
100 freestyle	53–56	1.80–2.05
200 freestyle	48–54	2.10–2.20
400/500 freestyle	42–55	1.75–2.20
800/1,000 freestyle	44–54	1.75–2.10
1,500/1,650 freestyle	N/A	N/A
100 backstroke	50–56	1.75–2.03
200 backstroke	42–40	1.90–2.08
100 breaststroke	47–53	1.60–1.90
200 breaststroke	34–45	1.97–2.48
100 butterfly	52–56	1.77–1.85
200 butterfly	45–54	1.74–1.90
MEN		
50 freestyle	56–67	1.88–2.16
100 freestyle	50–56	2.17–2.50
200 freestyle	43–51	2.25–2.41
400/500 freestyle	38–46	2.20–2.60
800/1,000 freestyle	N/A	N/A
1,500/1,650 freestyle	39–43	2.26–2.53
100 backstroke	48–53	2.05–2.20
200 backstroke	42–44	2.27–2.46
100 breaststroke	52–55	1.50–1.88
200 breaststroke	38–42	2.14–2.28
100 butterfly	52–56	1.90–2.15
200 butterfly	48–54	1.91–2.18

Fig 80 The range of stroke rates and stroke lengths for male and female world-class swimmers in each competitive event.

CHAPTER 19

TAPERING FOR PEAK PERFORMANCE

One of the most common discussion topics among swimming coaches is tapering for important competitions. The ultimate concept of tapering is a legacy of an outmoded training model that is gradually being replaced as coaches embrace periodized training principles. However, there still is a need for swimmers to recover from extensive periods of general and specific fatigue so that all the body's resources can be applied to competitive events.

The coaching strategy of working athletes hard and keeping them fatigued for many months was shown to be useful in the days when training usually did not fully stimulate or tax the physical capacities of individuals. As 'hard work' seemed to pay off, coaches logically assumed that, if hard work produced desirable results, more and harder work would produce even better results. In swimming and, indeed, in sports in general, that approach has been taken to extremes and is no longer supported by research evidence or the practices of very successful coaches and athletes. The British Swimming team (under the guidance of coach Bill Sweetenham) operates a strict set of guidelines for competition performances with targets set at 3 per cent, 2 per cent or 1 per cent above lifetime best according to training status, competition emphasis and cyclical planning. This ensures that, even at their most tired, in the hardest phase of training, swimmers have to perform very close to their best.

For many years swimming coaches believed that, although swimmers were always tired, training hard, and performances were not changing or were even deteriorating, good things were still happening. This was not the case. Better swimmers come from periodized programmes, with demonstrable training effects being derived from the judicious use of work and recovery throughout the year. However, there are still significant benefits to be gained from fine-tuning the preparation in the lead-up to the major competition(s) of the season, in other words, in the tapering period.

How Tapering Works

Two basic research findings should govern the underlying considerations for developing a taper:

1 Many coaches fear a loss of conditioning and performance if training is reduced for a long period (at least two or three weeks) before a major competition. Research has, however, shown that physiological gains achieved through extensive training are retained even when work volumes are reduced by amounts greater than one half. For some capacities, such as strength, the volume can be reduced to one-tenth and the capacity level will still be retained. Even days off are helpful.
2 The major benefit from a taper is the recovery and restoration that it facilitates. The feature that actually influences the competitive performance is the quality and type of training that has preceded the taper. A competitive performance is best considered to be an indication of the training programme that the athlete has experienced, not some magical activity that occurred during the taper. The nature of long-term training governs the type and level of performance that will be exhibited in serious competitions. If that investment is not correct and ultimately specific, high-level performances will not ensue, no matter how effective the taper.

These two principles set the two basic guidelines for tapering:

1 Allow rest and recovery to occur fully without confounding the procedure with the fear that conditioning will be lost; and
2 Perform specific performance tasks that will replicate the demands of the intended competitive effort.

One modern interpretation of why tapering works asserts that only neuromuscular and psychological factors recover; in other words, there is little or no change in physiological status. In a taper, neural and cognitive capacities increase in efficiency. Strength and power (neuromuscular functions) increase markedly, and the propelling efficiency of strokes (largely a cognitive recovery function) also increases. For these reasons, it is futile to attempt to get 'extra' physiological capacities during a taper. Its programming should allow neural and cognitive performance factors to recover and become more finely tuned.

Length of Taper

Research at the International Center for Aquatic Research (ICAR) has shown the maximum length of a taper to be three weeks, with the possibility of it being extended to four weeks. There are a number of factors which modify the actual length:

• There is considerable individuality in the tapering response. It should not be assumed that a planned taper will be appropriate for all swimmers. For those who recover very quickly during a 'group' taper it may be necessary to re-institute several days of quality training to delay the peaked state. While that form of training is being followed by some, others might be working lightly as their slower recovery occurs. A coach must be prepared to offer varied programmes for at least sub-groups of swimmers so that peaked performances will occur according to individual needs.

- The competitive schedule of the swimmer will also determine when a taper should start and what are programmed as training items. For a swimmer who will compete in the most important event on the fourth day of a championships, the taper should start later than one who has to compete on the first day. However, the opportunity to do controlled convenient swimming is rarely afforded at championship meets. The nature of the work that can be done over the crucial last three or four days at the competition site may require compromised planning. Usually, the commencement of the taper should be delayed even longer if quality work and volume cannot be fully exploited at the competitive arena, because of the extended rest that will occur there.
- The length of time that a swimmer has been in hard training is proportional to the length of time allocated to a taper. When a season of training is uninterrupted, the taper will be longest. However, when interruptions occur – for example, when a swimmer is selected for a trip abroad, goes on holiday, or is injured or ill – those interruptions should affect the length of a taper. Generally, it can be assumed that the closer the interruption to a championship meet, the shorter the taper period.

After the recommended maximum of three weeks for a taper, performance potential gradually decreases due to the less than adequate volume of event-specific training. Performance standards can remain very high past the three-week period but the swimmer gradually loses important performance capacities.

KEY POINT

The general length of a taper should be three weeks but certain events can intervene and warrant a shortening of its duration.

It is possible to extend the effects of a taper by alternating short bursts of intense training (actions that re-stimulate the specifically prepared physiological and biomechanical functions) with recovery. This occurs when there are a number of important swimming competitions in close proximity. In 2002, for example, the Commonwealth Games in Manchester were followed within a month by the Pan Pacific Championships in Japan and the Australian Short-Course Championships. Apart from coping with the demands of travelling across the globe, the swimmers who took part in all three competitions were able to sustain such a high level of performance that they were still breaking records on the final day of swimming in Melbourne. That demanding schedule of competitive experiences required at least maintenance physical training to occur in the intervening time period.

KEY POINT

Taper effects can be extended by the judicious use of quality training stimuli on a maintenance training schedule.

Volume of Work

The volume of work in a taper should be reduced to at least 60 per cent of that which existed during heavy training. However, for programmes that have had excessive volumes of training (for example, eleven sessions per week, 12km per day), the reduction could be to a level even below this. The principle of individuality has to be considered as a

major moderating variable for determining the appropriate length of the training volume reduction. Higher-volume training in the days immediately preceding an event may be detrimental to performance while a slow decay in volume will have a beneficial effect on maximizing competition preparation.

Some form of consistent performance measurement on at least an alternate-day schedule can be performed without any undue effect on competition performances. Times should be expected to improve gradually as the taper progresses.

The nature of the volume reduction should be by session. Eleven training sessions a week should gradually be reduced to about half this number. It is wrong to continue an excessive number of sessions while performing smaller training session loads, but eliminating all morning sessions from the schedule would be a fundamental error. Swimmers need to be able to swim fast in both morning (heat) and evening (semi-final or final) races.

There are a number of reasons why sessions should be reduced:

- the sessions off allow for greater recovery and energy restoration;
- the added rest time allows stresses from sources other than swimming to be tolerated; and
- there is a greater potential for restorative sleep to occur.

KEY POINT

The number of training sessions should be reduced in a taper rather than reducing session loads.

The correct nature of the volume decrease is not clear from the research or from the practice of successful coaches. Neither a stepwise nor a sudden decrease in volume appears to be any better than the other.

Specificity of Training and Taper Activities

It is suggested that tapering really only allows recovery and that final performances are related more to the type of training that precedes it rather than what is done in the taper itself. Anything that happens during a taper is unlikely to override the conditioned strength of responses developed through very extended periods of demanding training requiring specific adaptations.

KEY POINT

The major purpose of a taper is to allow athletes to recover from various forms of fatigue.

The most important variable for influencing competition performance is the specificity of the work that precedes the taper. That work should have the following characteristics:

- it should be of the same pace as the anticipated performance level so that biomechanical patterns can be refined under varying levels of fatigue;
- it should be of the same energy demand ratio (aerobic:anaerobic) as that demanded in each event; and
- it should require the same psychological control functions that will be needed in each race.

If a swimmer has several events, then each should be trained for specifically. A taper should continue specific training stimuli and should eliminate all non-specific demanding training experiences. Doing other activities in taper is a waste of time and may impede recovery benefits. There is no empirical support for any form of cross-training in a taper.

Non-specific training (for example, slow swimming, kicking, use of swimming paddles, flippers and so on) should only be used to provide variety and low-demand recovery activities. During a taper, the body should become highly sensitized to the specific qualities required for targeted events and desensitized to irrelevant activities. That desensitization is important. When a swimmer is tired in a race, the body has to determine which established forms of activity will be recruited to assist in performance maintenance. If there are slow-swimming patterns that are high in conditioned strength, they will be recruited and performance will suffer. If the body only knows fast-swimming patterns, then its selection options are limited to them and, consequently, fast swimming will be maintained. The activities programmed in the taper should always reinforce race-specific movement patterns and energy use.

If a swimmer intends to contest several races seriously, the demands of training (and subsequently of tapering) will be more complex, as the set 'paces' of all events should be trained. The difficulty with meeting this criterion is that excessive training is possible when ideally the training load of the taper should be reduced incrementally. To compromise this dilemma, any paces that are common to several events should be accommodated before a pace that is unique to a single event. Event preferences will also determine the importance of the selected specific training paces in the taper phase.

KEY POINT

The work performed in a taper should either be race-specific quality or of a recovery nature.

A taper will allow the emergence of the specific training effects that have occurred, particularly in the late specific preparatory and pre-competition training phases. The continuation of only race-specific training will heighten an athlete's (and the body's) awareness of the qualities of race requirements. That heightened sensitivity will increase the consistency of competition performance quality. Broken swims are a common way of ensuring that swimmers remain 'on task' during a taper.

Improvements During the Taper

Research indicates that improvements in performance during taper occur without changes in VO_2max. This suggests that the primary physiological changes are likely to be associated with adaptations at the muscular level rather than with oxygen delivery. Measuring VO_2max does not adequately reflect the positive effects of tapering in swimmers. Taper does not appear to affect sub-maximal post-exercise measurements (lactate, pH, bicarbonate, base excess) and heart rate. Blood measures have not been conclusively documented as being related to the taper phenomenon and, although not measured in swimmers, muscle glycogen and oxidative mechanisms have both been observed to increase in tapers in other sports.

The main performance attribute that changes during a taper is power. Consistent measurement of power, by performing short-distance time trials, can be used to indicate the positive effects of a taper to swimmers.

KEY POINT

Improvement in power is probably the major factor responsible for the improvement in competitive swimming performance through taper.

If it is too late to attempt to correct any physically conditioned state or biomechanical flaw during a taper, and it is detrimental to institute a short period of intense quality training in the belief that a 'little more' physical capability will be developed, the only option for training during a taper is specific work that yields positive affirmations of a swimmer's readiness.

Psychological factors are the major ingredients of performance that can be changed and improved during a taper. Positive thinking, self-concept, self-efficacy and performance predictions should be developed in order to foster a healthy approach to recovery and the impending competition. Mental-skills development and refinement are the major activities of tapering that will have the most direct transfer to the competitive situation. A significant amount of time at training, and in particular at the competition site, should be spent honing mental control skills, for example, practising activities such as warm-ups for specific races, focusing, controlling simulated race segments, evaluating segment goals, and rehearsing mental control content. A large section of tapering content should focus on psychological skills, specific mental control rehearsals, and the development of a group or team orientation.

Moderating Factors

There are a number of other factors that moderate the effects of a taper and warrant adjustments in planning.

Age

Young swimmers require a shorter taper period than older swimmers. Growing children and adolescents tire and recover more quickly than mature adults. Adjustments in taper lengths should be made according to the developmental age of each swimmer.

Eating and Drinking

With the reduced load (energy demand) associated with tapering, swimmers have to reduce their food intake. If normal eating habits and volumes are maintained, weight gains are possible, which, although minor, could have a slight detrimental effect on the swimmer.

The first stage of a taper often produces a 'bloated' feeling because of extra water retention in the muscles. For every gram of glycogen, 3g of water is stored. This often produces a feeling of heaviness or sluggishness.

There should be an increase in the number of high-carbohydrate meals as the competition time nears. This 'loading' should begin before travel and be maintained throughout the entire pre-competition and competition period. A high-carbohydrate diet will assist the athlete to tolerate stress.

STAR TIP

'Shaving' down' has been shown to have mechanical and consequent physiological benefits, as well as the less tangible, psychological boost of feeling more 'sleek' in the water.

Dealing with Stress

Athletes will usually increase their own internally generated pressures to improve performance. The more important the competition, the greater the level of self-imposed pressure. Since all athletes have a limited capacity for handling pressure, it is usually wise to attempt to reduce external stresses (those that come from parents, officials, the media, the coach) so that total pressure is manageable.

One important psychological theme of a taper and competition preparation is the removal of uncertainty. This can be achieved if the coach increases his own level of planning and communication. The better a swimmer is made aware of what will happen and how things will be organized, the less stressful the impending travel and competitions will be. If the coach changes to a noticeable elevation in preparedness and communication, a positive model will be provided for the athletes.

Competition Timings

The pattern of daily activity that is established in the body – circadian rhythm – through normal training usually does not match the timing of activities at a serious swimming meet. Circadian rhythms significantly affect the ability of an individual to perform at a particular time. Adjusting training times to better match the timing of activity that will occur at the competition, as well as time changes that occur through travel, is something that should be programmed. When times for heats and finals are known and time adjustments made, training at those times is desirable before going to the competition.

KEY POINT

Circadian rhythms need to be synchronized with the demands of the competitive schedule for maximum performances to be achieved.

Considerations for Coaches

A taper period and competition preparation phase are undoubtedly stressful for athletes but can be equally stressful for coaches. The coach should establish a heightened self-monitoring of his decisions, programmes and actions. Radical alterations in behaviour can signal panic to swimmers, which, in turn, could destroy their confidence and self-efficacy.

To ensure that the coach is a constructive rather than inappropriate model, the following issues should be contemplated daily:

- With regard to the type of swimming that is being performed, to what is the swimmer's body adapting? Non-specific work will have no value and can be counterproductive. Setting swims at 90 per cent intensity is meaningless to the body. The swimmer's mind may be aware of the intention, but the body will only practise the neuromuscular patterns and stimulate the energy supply that facilitates performing at that speed, which is slower than race pace. Only race-specific paces that require exact energy components and stimulate competition-specific mental control will have beneficial effects on performance. Any other form of swimming should be used for recovery purposes and should not be associated with serious intentions.

KEY POINT

All non-specific training activities should be removed so that maladaptation will not occur.

- Are each swimmer's personal needs being accommodated? Be prepared to rest swimmers at odd times, to programme separate activities, and to attend to personal requirements. The taper is too critical to persist with the convenience of group programming. During a taper and at competitions, coaches have to be prepared to work harder than normal, for individualized attention and programming are more demanding than singular group control actions.
- What assessment swims have been performed to detect lazy or over-zealous swimmers? Gradual recovery, with increasingly better levels of performance, particularly in activities that require a power component, should be expected. If changes are too

rapid, then a slowing of the improvement might be achieved by increasing the daily training load. If performances are poor, even though increased rest has been programmed, malingering or outside-of-swimming intrusions should be investigated. Measurement is an essential feature for judging tapering progress. It will not consume a swimmer's potential to perform well in a race. A common means of doing this employed by swimmers and coaches is to perform short sections of key test sets used throughout the season to mark progress or race readiness, for example, 5 x 100 or 3 x 200, measuring times/splits/stroke rates and finishing heart rate, and so on.
- Have the swimmers been prepared to do warm-ups, recovery routines, and race simulations before travelling to the competition? A coach should not be afraid to perform event simulations prior to important meets. If an athlete is not practised at performing between-event recovery routines, he cannot be expected to be proficient at doing them under the stress of competition. There is a real programming need to perform these activities as part of normal training in the pre-competition and taper phases.

KEY POINT

Since swimmers are asked to alter their behaviours and become more serious as a competition approaches, the coach should model those expectations by improved behaviours, planning, self-control, and provision of individual attention.

Summary

The taper has traditionally been given more credit than it deserves for affecting performance. It is primarily a period that allows recovery, restitution, specific practice refinements, and planning of competition behaviours. What will be exhibited in races are the beneficial effects of training that has been done prior to the taper.

The psychological activity and state of the athlete becomes increasingly important as the taper progresses and should be the primary focus of the programme. It is incorrect to think that skills can be altered in any beneficial manner or that extra physical condition can be gained by short bouts of intense training. By the time a taper is started, it is too late to consider any biomechanical or physiological change training. As the taper progresses, indications that performance is improving and that competition conduct activities are being practised, will have a beneficial effect on the athlete's psychological state. If events are predictable, practised, and accompanied by a self-efficacy of performance excellence, then a successful competition is likely.

The role of the coach as the model of seriousness, control, planning and professional competence is important for swimmers if they are expected to perform in a similar manner. Positive and constructive coaching, and exhibiting a capacity to cope with any problem in a competent manner, will contribute to athletes believing that all conditions exist for them to perform well.

PART 5

HOW TO FIND OUT MORE

CHAPTER 20

STRUCTURE AND ORGANIZATION OF SWIMMING

Swimming in Great Britain is organized like most other sports. There is an international structure (FINA), which organizes international competitions, rules and so on, as well as a number of National Governing Bodies (NGBs), which are responsible for the sport in each home country.

The umbrella body for swimming in Great Britain is British Swimming. As well as being responsible for the sport of Swimming, British Swimming is also accountable for the development of Diving, Synchronized Swimming, Water Polo and Open Water. Its main function is to take charge of the

international high-performance aspects of each discipline. The primary members of British Swimming are the three home-nation governing bodies of England (Amateur Swimming Association), Scotland (Scottish Swimming) and Wales (Welsh Amateur Swimming Association).

Fig 81 The structure of swimming.

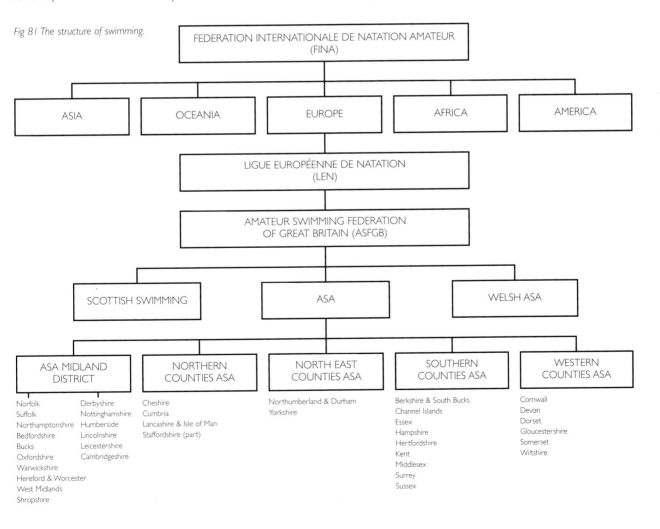

USEFUL ADDRESSES

National Governing Bodies

British Swimming and English ASA
Harold Fern House
Derby Square
Loughborough
Leicestershire, LE11 5AL
Tel: 01509 618700
Fax: 01509 618701
email: cserv@asagb.org.uk

Irish ASA
House of Sport
Longmile Road
Dublin 12
Eire
Tel: 00 353 1 450 1739
Fax: 00 353 1 450 2805
email: webmaster1@swimireland.ie

Scottish Swimming
National Swimming Academy
University of Stirling
Stirling
FK9 4LA
Tel: 01786 466520
Fax: 01786 466521
email: info@scottishswimming.com

Welsh ASA
Wales National Pool Swansea
Sketty Lane
Swansea
SA2 8QG
Tel: 01792 513636
Fax: 01792 513637
email: secretary@welshasa.co.uk

Swimming/Natation Canada
2197 Riverside Drive, Suite 700
Ottawa, Ontario K1H 7X3
Canada
Tel: 613 260 1348
Fax: 613 260 0804
email: natloffice@swimming.ca

United States Swimming, Inc.
One Olympic Plaza
Colorado Springs CO 80909
USA
Tel: 719 866 4578
Fax: 719 866 4761
email: webmaster@usa-swimming.org

South Africa (RSA)
Swimming South Africa
Johannesburg Athletic Stadium
124 Van Beek Street
North Wing, Ground Floor
2094 New Doornfontein
Johannesburg
South Africa
Tel: 27-11 404 2480
Fax: 27 11 402 2481
email: gensec@swimsa.co.za

Australia (AUS)
Australian Swimming Ltd
Unit 12, 7 Beissel Street
Belconnen Act 2617
PO Box 3286
Canberra
Australia
Tel: 61-2 6219 5600
Fax: 61-2 6219 5606
email: swim@swimming.org.au

New Zealand (NZL)
Swimming New Zealand
Level 3, Booth House
202–206 Cuba Street
PO Box 11 115
Wellington
New Zealand
Tel: 64-4 801 9450
Fax: 64-4 801 6270
email: sport@swimmingnz.org.nz

Other Bodies

ISTC (Institute of Swimming Teachers & Coaches)
41 Granby Street
Loughborough
Leicestershire, LE11 3DU
Tel: 01509 264357
email: istc@swimming.org.uk

FINA (Fédération Internationale de Natation Amateur)
Avenue de L'Avant – Poste 4
1005 Lausanne
Switzerland
Tel: 41 21 310 4710
Fax: 41 21 312 6610
web: www.fina.org

BSCTA (British Swimming Coaches & Teachers Association)
Brian McGuinness, Secretary
Will Thorne House
2 Birmingham Road
Halesowen
West Midlands, B63 3HP
Tel: 0121 550 4888
Fax: 0121 550 4272
email: brian.mcguinness@gmb.org.uk

LEN (Ligue Européenne de Natation)
c/o C.O.N.I., Stadio Olympico
Palazzina Bonifati
00/94 Roma, Italy
Tel: 39 06 3685 7870
Fax: 39 06 3237058
email: lenoffice@tin.it

GLOSSARY

This is a glossary of words and terms used in this book and in the sport of swimming. You may or may not find these words in the English Dictionary, and if you do, their definitions will probably be radically different from the ones given here.

Accredited meet   A meet conducted with sufficient officials to certify conformance to the rules.

Admission   Certain meets charge for spectators to view the meets. These are usually the larger, more prestigious meets. Sometimes the meet programme (start sheet) is included in the price of admission.

Aggregate time   Times achieved by four swimmers in individual events that are added together to arrive at a relay entry time.

Anchor leg   The final swimmer in a relay.

ASCA   The American Swimming Coaches Association.

Backstroke   One of the four competitive racing strokes, basically any style of swimming on the back. Backstroke is swum as the first stroke in the Medley Relay and second stroke in the IM.

Beep   The starting sound from an electronic, computerized timing system.

Blocks   The starting platforms located behind each lane. Some pools have blocks at the deeper end of the pool, and some have blocks at both ends. Blocks have a variety of designs and can be permanent or removable.

Breaststroke   One of the four competitive racing strokes. Breaststroke is swum as the second stroke in the Medley Relay and the third stroke in the IM.

BSCTA   The British Swimming Coaches and Teachers Association

Bulletin   One of the most important communication devices for a swim club. Bulletin boards are usually in the entrance ways of pools and have timely information posted for swimmers and parents to read.

Butterfly   One of the four competitive racing strokes. Butterfly (or 'Fly') is swum as the third stroke in the Medley Relay and first stroke in the IM.

Button   The manual timing-system stopping device that records a back-up time in case the touch pad malfunctioned. The button is at the end of a wire, plugged into a deck terminal box. There are usually two or three buttons per lane. It is the timekeeper's responsibility to push the button as the swimmer finishes the race.

Carbohydrates   The main source of food energy used by athletes.

Cards   A card that may either be handed to the swimmer or given to the timekeeper behind the lane. Cards usually list the swimmer's name, competitor number, seed time, event number, event description, and the lane and heat number the swimmer will swim in. Backup times are written on these cards. Each event may have a separate card.

Championship finals   Race run between the top six or eight swimmers (depending on the number of pool lanes) from the heats swim at a championship meet. The fastest heat of finals when multiple heats are held.

Championship meet   The meet held at the end of a season. Qualification times are usually necessary to enter meet.

Cycle seeding   A method of seeding swimmers when they are participating in a heats/finals event. The fastest eighteen to twenty-four swimmers are seeded in the last three heats, with the fastest swimmers being in the inside lanes.

Clinic   A scheduled meeting for the purpose of education/instruction, for example, of officials, coaches and so on.

Club   A registered swimming organization within the NGB.

Code of Ethics   A code of conduct that both swimmers and coaches are required to sign for certain events.

Course   Designated distance (length of pool) for swimming competition.

Deadline   The date meet entries must be received by, to be accepted by the meet host. Making the meet deadline does not guarantee acceptance into a meet since many meets are 'full' weeks before the entry deadline.

Deck   The area around the swimming pool reserved for swimmers, officials and coaches.

Deck entries   Entries accepted into swimming events on the first or later day of a meet.

Dehydration   The abnormal depletion of body fluids (water). The most common cause of swimmer's cramps and sick feelings.

Development meet   A classification of meet or competition that is usually held early in the season. The purpose of a development meet is to allow all levels of swimmers to compete in a low-pressure environment.

Disqualification   The discounting of a swimmer's performance because of a rules infraction. A disqualification is shown by an official raising one arm with open hand above the head.

Dive   Head-first entry into the water. Diving is not allowed during warm-ups except at the designated time, in specific lanes that are monitored by the swimmer's coach or designated personnel.

Diving pool   A separate pool or a pool set off to the side of the competition pool, with deeper water and diving boards/platforms. During a meet, this area may be designated as a warm-down pool, with proper supervision.

Drop-off time   The differential between split times for both halves of a race.

Dryland   The exercises and various strength programmes swimmers do out of the water.

Dual meet   Meet at which two teams/clubs compete against each other.

Electronic timing   Timing system, usually with touch pads in the water, junction boxes on the deck with hook-up cables, buttons for backup timing, and a computer-type console that prints out the results of each race. Some systems are hooked up to a scoreboard that displays swimmers' names.

Entry An individual, relay team, or club roster's event list into a swim competition.

Entry fee The amount per event a swimmer or relay is charged.

Entry limit Each meet will usually have a limit of total swimmers they can accept, or a time limit they cannot exceed. Once an entry limit has been reached, a meet will be closed and all other entries returned.

Equipment The items necessary to operate a swimming session or conduct a competition.

Event A race or stroke over a given distance. An event equals one heat with its final, or one timed final.

False start When a swimmer leaves the starting block before the horn or gun. One false start will disqualify a swimmer or a relay team, although the starter or referee may disallow the false start due to unusual circumstances.

False start rope A recall rope across the width of the racing pool for the purpose of stopping swimmers who were not aware of a false start. The rope is placed 15m from the start end.

Fastest to slowest A seeding method used on the longer events held at the end of a session. The fastest seeded swimmers participate in the first heats followed by the next fastest, and so on. Often, these events will alternate girls' and boys' heats until all swimmers have competed.

Fees Money paid by swimmers for services, for example, monthly coaching fees.

FINA The international, rules-making organization, governing the sport of swimming.

Final The last race of each event, contested between the top swimmers from the heats.

Final results The printed copy of the results of each race of a swim meet.

Fine The monetary penalty imposed upon a swimmer or club when a swimmer does not achieve the necessary time required in an event.

Fins Sometimes known as 'flippers', rubber devices that fit on a swimmer's feet, used in swim practice, not competition.

Flags Markers suspended over the width of each end of the pool 5m from the wall to guide backstroke swimmers to the wall.

Freestyle One of the four competitive racing strokes. Freestyle (or 'Free') is swum as the fourth stroke in the Medley Relay and fourth stroke in the IM.

Gallery The viewing area for spectators during the swimming competition.

Goals The short- and long-range targets for swimmers to aim for.

Goggles Glasses-type devices worn by swimmers to protect their eyes from being irritated by the chlorine in the water.

Heats A division of an event when there are too many swimmers to compete at the same time. The results are compiled according to swimmers' times swum, after all heats of the event are completed.

IM Individual Medley. A swimming event using all four of the competitive strokes on consecutive lengths of the race, in the order Butterfly, Backstroke, Breaststroke, Freestyle. Equal distances must be swum of each stroke.

Interval A specific elapsed time for swimming or rest, used during swim practice.

Kick board A flotation device used by swimmers during training for legs-only practices.

Lane lines Continuous floating markers attached to a cable stretched from the starting end to the turning end for the purpose of separating each lane and quieting the waves caused by racing swimmers.

Lap One length of the course. Sometimes may also mean down and back (two lengths) of the pool.

Lap counter The large numbered cards used during the 800m and 1,500m Freestyle events.

Leg The part of a relay event swum by a single team member. A single stroke in the IM.

Length The extent of the competitive course from end to end.

Long-course A 50m pool.

Mark 'Take your mark' is the command to the swimmer to take his starting position.

Marshal The adult(s) (official) who controls the crowd and swimmer flow at a swim meet.

Meet A series of events held in one programme.

Meet director The official in charge of the administration of a meet.

Metres The measurement of the length of a swimming pool that was built per specs using the metric system. Long-course is 50m, short-course is 25m.

Mile (US) Slang term referring to the 1,500m Freestyle.

NAGs National Age Group Championships, held annually.

Nationals National championships, held annually.

Negative split Referring to a swim paced with the second half faster than the first, as in 'he swam a negative 400, 2.02 and 1.59'.

NGB National governing body.

Officials The certified, adult volunteers, who operate the many facets of a swim competition.

Olympic trials The accredited long-course swim meet held the year of the Olympic Games to decide which swimmers will represent their country.

Omega A brand of automatic timing system.

Open competition Competition that any qualified club, organization, or individual may enter.

Pace clock Electronic clock with highly visible numbers and second hands, positioned at the ends or sides of a swimming pool so the swimmers can read their times during warm-ups or training sessions (sometimes called 'Sweep Clock').

Paddles Coloured plastic devices worn on the swimmer's hands during training.

Practice The scheduled workouts a swimmer attends with his swim team/club.

Prelims Session of a Prelims/Finals meet in which the qualification heats are conducted, otherwise known as 'heats'.

Pull buoy A flotation device used for pulling by swimmers in practice.

Qualifying times Published times necessary to enter certain meets, or the times necessary to achieve a specific category of swimmer.

INDEX

Race Any single swimming competition.

Ready room A pool-side room where swimmers marshal before competing.

Referee The head official at a swim meet in charge of all of the 'wet-side' administration and decisions.

Relay A swimming event in which four swimmers participate as a team, each one swimming an equal distance of the race. There are two types of relay: Medley (with one swimmer swimming backstroke, one swimming breaststroke, one swimming butterfly, one swimming freestyle, in that order), and Freestyle, in which all four swimmers swim freestyle.

Rest area A designated area (such as a gymnasium) that is set aside for swimmers to rest during a meet.

Seed Assigning the swimmers' heats and lanes according to their submitted or preliminary times.

Senior meet A meet that is for senior-level swimmers, not divided into age groups. Qualification times are usually necessary and will vary depending on the level of the meet.

Session Portion of meet distinctly separated from other portions by locale, time, type of competition, or age group.

Short-course A 25m pool.

Split A portion of an event, shorter than the total distance, that is timed, for example, a swimmer's first 50 time is taken as the swimmer swims the 100 race. It is common to take multiple splits for the longer distances.

Start The beginning of a race or the dive used to begin a race.

Starter The official in charge of signalling the beginning of a race and ensuring that all swimmers have a fair take-off.

Stations Separate portions of a dry-land or weight circuit.

Stroke There are four competitive strokes: Butterfly, Backstroke, Breaststroke, Freestyle.

Stroke judge The official positioned at the side of the pool, walking the length of the course as the swimmers race. If the stroke judge sees something illegal, it is reported to the referee and the swimmer may be disqualified.

Submitted time Times used to enter swimmers in meets. These times must have been achieved by the swimmer at previous meets.

Swim-down The 'recovery swimming' a swimmer does after a race when pool space is available.

Swim-off In a heat/finals-type competition, a race after the scheduled event to break a tie. The only circumstance that warrants a swim-off is when it is necessary to determine which swimmer will make a final.

Taper The resting phase of a senior swimmer at the end of the season before the championship meet.

Time trial An event or series of events in which a swimmer may achieve or better a required time standard.

Timekeeper The volunteers sitting behind the starting blocks/finish end of the pool, who are responsible for getting watch times on events and activating the back-up buttons for the timing system.

Touch pad The removable plate (on the end of the pool) that is connected to an automatic timing system. A swimmer must properly touch the touch pad to register an official time in a race.

Unofficial time The time displayed on a read-out board or read over the intercom by the announcer immediately after the race. After the time has been checked, it will become the official time.

Warm-up The practice and 'loosening-up' session a swimmer does before the meet or their event is swum.

Whistle The sound a starter/referee makes to signal for quiet before giving the command to start the race.

Yardage The distance a swimmer races or swims in practice. Total yardage can be calculated for each practice session.

Yards The measurement of the length of a swimming pool that was built per specs using the American system. A short-course yard pool is 25 yards (75ft) in length.